AF595867

The People Pleaser's Guide to

Saying Yes to You

HOLLIE AZZOPARDI

First published by Affirm Press in 2025
Bunurong/Boon Wurrung Country
28 Thistlethwaite Street
South Melbourne VIC 3205
affirmpress.com.au

10 9 8 7 6 5 4 3 2 1

Affirm Press is located on the unceded land of the Bunurong/Boon Wurrung peoples of the Kulin Nation. Affirm Press pays respect to their Elders past and present.

The author acknowledges the Traditional Owners of the land on which this book was written, the Arakwal people of the Bundjalung Nation, and pays respect to their Elders past and present.

The information in this book is general in nature. Please consult your healthcare practitioner before making any dietary or lifestyle changes, to ensure you choose the approach that works best for you.

A catalogue record for this book is available from the National Library of Australia

ISBN: 9781923046863 (hardback)

Cover design by Georgie Sweeting © Affirm Press
Back cover author photograph by Shannon Kelly/Light of Mine Photography
Internal design by Post Pre-press Group, Brisbane
Printed and bound in China by C&C Offset Printing Co. Ltd.

For the little girl inside of me, praying for her life to change.

We did it.

Contents

Introduction

It seems fitting that the week I was approached to write this book was also the week I had one of my biggest meltdowns in the last two years of navigating new motherhood.

After a month of overwhelming obligations – two Sydney trips for weddings (with my toddler in tow both times), gastro from first said trip wiping out our household for a week, paid work that still needed to be done, dishes that still needed washing, a dog that seizured after we promised our pet-sitter he wouldn't (sorry Tia!) and finally, the grand crescendo, a pairing of threadworms and fevers for my little girl after our second Sydney trip – it's really no wonder I found myself hyperventilating into the phone at 1.30am, asking my mum to help me find my centre again; because … where the fuck did she go? Where did *I* go?

My initiation into motherhood is really summed up in that question: *where did I go?*

It seems that even those of us who know better don't necessarily do better.

I wrote my first book on people-pleasing and putting yourself first during one of the happiest, easiest times of my life. Heck, I gloat about it in the book. How aligned I felt. How in-flow life was. How easily everything came to me. And it's still true – everything I shared in that book, every lesson I learned, every activity I shared – I stand by it all. I was a different version of myself when I wrote those words.

But the Hollie writing this book today is far from the Hollie who wrote that first book only three years ago. I've changed. And that is the only real constant in life. (Well, that and death, but let's ease into things, shall we?)

It's taken a whole lot of forgetting who I am, forging new identities and saying yes to myself in entirely new, deep and unfathomable ways to land here, writing this today.

Decisions I thought I'd never have to make. Relationships I thought I'd never have to end. Masks I thought I'd never take off. All crumbling around me, leaving behind a raw, vulnerable and authentic truth standing in the ruins of who I was, not yet fully embodied in who I will become. And somehow, for all the rubble, feeling better, lighter and so much shinier.

This is a book about saying yes to you, no matter the season of life you are navigating. Because here's the thing: life will life (you can quote me on that). And there will be times when it feels absolutely impossible to 'put yourself first'. I hear you. So when we find ourselves in these moments, instead of putting ourselves first, how can we simply say YES to ourselves more?

Even with the dishes piling in the sink and the work still needing to be done after a full day of mothering a sick toddler – how can we say yes to ourselves?

Even with the two interstate weddings back-to-back, the social obligations and financial strain – how can we say yes to ourselves?

Even when our thyroid is inflamed, our nervous system is maxed out and our birth trauma is birth-trauma-ing – how can we say yes to ourselves?

These are all questions I continue to ask myself, standing on the other side of the greatest initiation of my life. The ego deaths, the identity crumblings, the doing of things I'd sworn I'd 'never do' … I've been left with more questions than answers. I've felt immense shame at the judgements I once held against other people when I found myself right there in their shoes for the first time ever. Suddenly every 'truth' I'd ever known became more fiction than fact, leaving a trail of blurry lines and uncertainty behind me.

But despite all of the unknowns, what I know for certain? This isn't failure.

THIS is where growth lives. THIS is where truth lives. THIS is the raw and vulnerable thread that leads us right to the heart of it.

So, how do we make sense of it all? How do we finally say YES to ourselves – our lives, our dreams, our biggest, truest visions?

First, it's time to peel back the layers of identity to what lies beneath. To remember – or perhaps discover for the first time ever – who we really, truly are. Because once we are clearer on this, clarity forms in all areas of our lives. We start to understand what it actually means to say yes to ourselves – because we understand what it means to truly BE ourselves.

From that place, we can start to slow down. Tune in. Reclaim who we are at our core; our deepest of truths, our boldest of dreams.

And from this place – we shine.

I can confidently say I have found my shine.

You can shine too, friend.

Let's hold hands and do it together.

Love, Hollie

SECTION 1

Say Yes (to You)

CHAPTER 1

Will the Real Hollie Please Stand Up?

I have an apology to make. It's one I have consistently made over the past two years; however, this is one I want printed in ink for all of you to read – perhaps over and over again, if you really need to hear it. This is an apology to all of the mothers who have walked before me who I didn't fully recognise until I became one myself.

I am sorry. I am so, so sorry.

I am sorry I didn't understand until I went through my own experience of becoming.

I am sorry I didn't advocate for you in my maidenhood. That I didn't cook for you, offer to clean, that I didn't just spend time with you doing a whole lot of nothing when the space in my life afforded me that opportunity.

I'm sorry I didn't understand the depths of all you navigated to become who you now are. I'm sorry I didn't get it. I'm sorry that I didn't know any different or any better. I am so sorry.

I find myself in moments of deep cringe when I reflect on the person I was when I wrote my first book. Perhaps cringe is too harsh a word. I have so much love for that version of me, don't get me wrong, but my gosh, the naivety! I don't think there's necessarily any way around it – the pure-hearted innocence that lives on the side before the 'unknown' – however, I will repeat it until I run out of breath: I am sorry. I am so sorry.

I think every mother can understand why I'm apologising, but maybe you're not a mother and maybe you never will be, and that's okay. This isn't a book about motherhood; it's a book about identity. Judgement. Ego death. Crumbling. All to find yourself again.

The point is that I am not who I was when I wrote my first book. And I'm not apologising for that version of me – far from it – but I feel it is only right to apologise for my blind spots. For the grand sweeping statements and assumptions that were only relevant to those in a similar position to me. For the spaces I didn't fill due to my unknowing.

I write this book a completely new version of myself. And not really from my own choosing, but due to the enormity of becoming a mother. Perhaps you are also navigating a different great life transition. Leaving a job that defined your sense of self for the longest time. Stepping into the truth of your sexual identity. Ending or beginning a new, deep, exciting and perhaps scary love story. Grieving the passing of a loved one. Discovering a relationship with spirituality. Eating meat for the first time in 20 years (I see you!). Whatever your 'big life' thing is, there is something incredibly powerful that lies on the other side of a mass crumbling. A huge becoming; a realisation of who you once were, and who you are now.

That's the thing about life – we aren't *supposed* to remain the same. Change is a huge point of fear for so many of us. But something we tend to forget is the liberation that lies on the other side of change. The freedom that change affords us. Those of us who cling desperately to fixed sameness, to never unravelling, to always remaining unchanged, are forever lost in ruminating nostalgia, living purely in the space of 'what was', repeating the same stories of better times gone by, ignoring the expanse of life right here in the present moment.

Or maybe you're on the flip side, shooting forth in your mind of 'what could be'. Which is absolutely okay as long as you're not just living in the space of your mind. Because without any solid change – without the identity crumbles, without the ego deaths, without the questioning of your own truths, of what makes you, you – will anything really change?

What I'm trying to say is without change, we cannot grow. Or even deeper than that: without change, we cannot live. Not fully. Not truly. Not madly, and absolutely not deeply. (And yes, I will happily stand with you on mountains and bathe with you in seas.)

The challenge is that mass life change likely comes with a side of upheaval. And who in their right mind is running towards that? I know I wasn't when my world came crumbling down. It's not something we actively seek out. But when it happens, rather than running from the fear of it all, we must try to lean *into* the experience, and rise from the ashes that have burned everything away, if we want to be more of who we are. We can use the flames as our ally, and walk as the alchemist of our own lives, knowing that, no matter what comes, no matter what part of us falls away, we will come out as more of who we truly are.

That is a life I want to live.

–

If you have read my first book, *The People Pleaser's Guide to Putting Yourself First*, you will know that I wrote that book during one of the happiest times of my life. I was experiencing a healthy, vibrant pregnancy with my first child, and writing my first book at the same time. We had recently made the move to our dream location in the countryside after 30+ years of city living, and honestly, if I shared a montage of that time, it would be set to 'Little Life' by Holly Storey, that soothing, soulful soundtrack everyone's frothing about on TikTok at the moment. Life felt simple and magic, and it was an easy space for me to sit and write about putting yourself first. That's not to dilute the hard work of that time too; however, the great irony of writing a book is that your work doesn't end once the words are written. Far from it. To be fully embodied in what you are teaching – at least as a non-fiction writer – life likes to hand you lessons to encourage you to step up to the plate. Practise what you preach. Walk the talk.

During that time, I had to make some big changes. I had some really touchy conversations with loved ones, and put boundaries in place I'd never wanted to before, all for the sake of embodying what I had written in my first book. I even had a friendship totally break down. It was hard. Uncomfortable. And also – incredibly expansive.

By the time my first book hit the shelves, my little girl was already celebrating her first birthday (such are the timelines of publishing!). So while everyone was reading about this spectacular time in my life, the truth is, only one year down the track, I was broken.

And that's putting it lightly.

My motherhood initiation was not an easy one.

A 47-hour posterior labour that saw me projectile vomiting nonstop, pumped with drips of saline, and ending with an epidural, my legs in stirrups, an episiotomy and forceps pulling my little girl from me while an emergency nurse from the NICU was on stand-by (and no hospital visitors because #Covid) followed by months on end of undetected low milk supply (because no one could visit because #Covid), navigating the Northern Rivers floods with a three-month-old, and then one of our best friends having a terrible accident that left him in a coma, and us not knowing if he would ever wake up …

Let's just say that life really got me in that first year of motherhood.

The picturesque hinterland drives were suddenly a source of anxiety preventing me from even leaving my driveway, lest my car-averse baby start screaming; my thriving, miraculous body was 'failing' me, my baby and my dreams to breastfeed her; and my chosen home environment had me isolated from any consistent support by way of friends and family at a time when I'd never needed help more in my life.

When people would tell me to 'enjoy the newborn bubble', I wanted to scream. When people told me the baby days went by so fast and to enjoy their sleepy cuddles, I was baffled. The days couldn't have been going slower. And what sleep? My baby was so hungry that there were multiple days in those first few weeks when I had her attached to my breasts for 18 hours a day. That's not writer's licence to exaggerate either; she would suckle constantly, and I would only move to pee. There was one particular night when we watched the sun set and rise again from the same spot in our bed, without either of us getting one minute of sleep.

It was the perfect storm. And only now – two years after the fact – can I look back on that time and see it for what it was: the greatest initiation of my life.

For months after my little girl's birth, I would catch my reflection in the mirror and genuinely not recognise who was staring back. There were moments in my highly distressed and sleep-deprived state that I actually wondered if this was a secret mothers kept; that after birth, your entire face changed. Not only did I not feel like myself, but I didn't look like myself either. I was staring at a total stranger. And in my ear, I had everyone telling me to 'enjoy this time' – and so the guilt I felt for not was overwhelming.

When my little girl was born, I didn't cry. I was relieved she was here, absolutely. In my wired state, I pulled up her birth chart to see her astrological signs while the doctor was stitching me up (20 stitches, in and out). (Sag Sun, Sag Moon, Libra Rising, by the way. I even joked about Scorpios with my obstetrician while he stitched me up because she had a Scorpio placement and – lo and behold – he was one.)

But I didn't feel that instant connection. The only instant pull I felt was: *fuck, I need to keep this child alive.* And at that point, I didn't even know how to keep myself alive.

Things got worse. That first year of motherhood was the darkest time of my life. And while I hold no shame in writing that, I do hold grief – I am crying as I write these words. I am saddened that our transition as a family was filled with such challenge, such turmoil. I am still affected when I hear of the joyous motherhood initiations that friends and strangers alike have experienced; even while I am happy for them, I feel acutely the unfairness that mine was plagued with such distress, such deep trauma, amounting to complex PTSD and a very real fear of ever having another child. Why did it go this way for us?

In owning the truth of this part of my journey, I really hope to alleviate the pressure any other person is placing on themselves for not experiencing the perfect initiation. Just because society tells you to 'enjoy this time' doesn't mean you have to, or that you're 'wrong' if you don't. I've always been the kind of person to reply honestly when someone asks how I am. If I'm having a shit time, I'll say, 'Yeah, I'm having a shit time.' It takes people aback. People aren't used to that level of directness, especially when it comes to our feelings. But I'm not one to slap a bumper sticker on the truth of my lived experiences.

And the truth is that first year of motherhood was the hardest year of my life. I hated most days of that year.

Our lives are a direct reflection of the truths we tell ourselves. If you tell yourself you're fine when you're feeling lost, confused, frustrated or angry, then you are telling yourself your very real, very human feelings are *not valid*. That you aren't allowed to feel because what would that mean? This is actually something so terrifying for so many of us. It feels far safer to dilute our feelings, to run from them, to not let them in. This is why so many of us live with closed hearts, why avoidant-attachment is a very real love language, why we find ourselves apologising for our moods and tears and why the thought of diving deep into any substantial therapy or healing feels 'too much'.

To feel deeply is absolutely terrifying. It requires a level of self-reflection and honesty that most people will walk their entire lives in the opposite direction to avoid.

But this is also what makes us human. Our capacity to feel deeply. To cry, to crumble, to feel so angry we might burst, to feel so much joy our cheeks hurt, to laugh to the point of peeing our pants, to jump for joy so hard at a Taylor Swift concert that you pee your pants (the peeing-pants thing is more common for me these days).

We are at a time where technological and artificial intelligence is surpassing our own. One of the key qualities that will never be replaced is our capacity to feel.

If we turn that off? Well, we might as well be robots.

I want to share a little poem I wrote when I was 13. I am literally opening the pages of my teenage journal for you all here, so please – go kindly. The poem is called 'Pretend'.

> What happened to me?
> You're so happy, do you ever cry?
> They always say,
> Do they know how it feels
> To pretend
> To want to be someone else
> Week after week

To dread the school bell to ring at the end of the day
No, they don't know what it's like
To cry every day
To come to school looking happy
But on the inside …
No one else is like that
Just me
They don't know what it's like
To pretend

If I could sit down with this version of me, today (and chances are, I will be doing this in some capacity ten years from now with my little mini-me) I would tell her this:

You are allowed to feel whatever you are feeling. I do not judge you for what you are feeling. You are safe to feel these things. You are safe to share openly what you are feeling. And please don't feel like you have to do this by yourself. There are so many people who love you, and want to help you. But you have to let them in. Pretending everything is okay is not the answer. In fact, that will deepen your wounds, your traumas, your challenges – making for more inner work later.

These feelings don't go anywhere. Our body stores them until the right moment arrives to move them through. Or perhaps when our body simply cannot hold anymore. Don't hold these feelings in. Share them with someone you trust. Find methods that feel safe. Move them through. Please, move them through.

During my first year of motherhood, I experienced compound trauma as a direct result of the accumulated traumas – and the associated feelings of these traumas – that I had not allowed myself to feel, dating back more than 20 years. Unbeknownst to me at the time I wrote the poem (I was 13, after all), every experience over the coming 20 years that I didn't admit to, share with someone or allow myself to express (because pretending I was happy and okay was far easier) was piling up. Then my motherhood transition created just enough space for a grand crescendo of rage, anger, fury, sadness and grief. A tidal wave of unprocessed traumas.

But let's go back a bit. What even *is* trauma? And how do we know if we have our own traumas stored in our bodies?

I sat down with Eleanor Danks, somatic therapist and sexual violence survivor, to discuss exactly what trauma is, and how we can navigate it when it becomes compounded, or complex.

> Trauma occurs when we experience a state of emotional distress to a degree that overwhelms our capacity to cope with and digest it. Included in this experience is usually also a real or perceived sense of helplessness, an inability to find a way out of it. The result of this is that an imprint of that distress – and the pain, helplessness and terror within it – continues to live inside us, and when triggered, that distress replays as if it is happening all over again in the present moment.
>
> There is no limit as to what an event or experience that results in trauma can look like. These experiences can be individual, relational, systemic or collective. They can happen directly to us or they can be something we witness happen to someone else. They can be experiences that are passed down through generations of family lines. What defines a traumatic experience and subsequent trauma is not

> the parameters of the event/s, but the distress that we experience as a result of it.
>
> … the amount and severity of trauma that each of us have experienced differs greatly, as well as how deeply and what ways it continues to affect our life now. For some, trauma will only affect us in very small and inconsequential ways. For others, the effects of trauma will be absolutely life-altering, devastating and widespread through all areas of our life.

The term 'complex trauma' was first coined by Dr Judith Lewis Herman and refers to a series of traumatic events that take place over a long period of time. Over years and years, unprocessed trauma upon unprocessed trauma piles on top of one another, building to a point where the enormity can no longer be held. Cue tidal wave. This can look like a torrent of unprocessed emotion being felt all at once (hello, deep-seated rage, nice to meet you) or, in many cases (myself included), a complete and utter breakdown.

Eleanor explains:

> Trauma can become 'complex' in two main ways. The first is when we experience trauma that continues over a long period of time, for example an abusive relationship or an ongoing debilitating illness. The second is when we experience trauma later in life that re-triggers an earlier trauma (most typically from our childhood).
>
> In both of these examples, what makes the trauma 'complex' is that multiple traumas become compounded upon and intertwined with one another. In addition to

this, it can also mean that other events that would not have otherwise been traumatic become so, due either to our capacity being overwhelmed more easily during a period of time, or because they become intertwined with the main traumatic experiences.

Complex trauma can be a severely debilitating and confusing experience, and it can make the effects of each trauma significantly greater than if they had happened in isolation. It also often results in the person losing their sense of self as well as their sense of trust in the world.

It was a few months into new motherhood when I realised something was wrong. I could no longer put what I was feeling down to sleep deprivation alone. I was angry. All the time. So angry that I was scared of what I would do with it. I'd never had that feeling before – like the rage needed somewhere to go – and being a stay-at-home mother, I had no outlet to move it through. I cried. A lot. More than I ever had before. My husband, Trent, was on shift work and we didn't have any help close by, so I spent hours upon hours on my own just sobbing, deep guttural wails.

I was isolated. I was alone. I was in deep pain, deep trauma and frightening levels of grief. The pain was like I was grieving someone who had died, yet no one had. I had just birthed new life, yet I'd never experienced such grief.

It got to a point where one day, while my little girl was asleep, I found myself in such a state of overwhelming anger that I threw one of her bottles against the wall. I'd never thrown anything in anger before in my life. I had vowed to never be one of those parents. And there I was, only a few months in, right in their shoes. It was the wake-up call I needed.

I promptly booked myself into a therapist, who very quickly recognised that I was experiencing a cumulation of complex trauma, compound PTSD and postnatal depression.

No wonder I felt so shit.

–

I don't do things in halves. I verge on addictive behaviour when it comes to my own personal development work and healing. Oftentimes, I go overboard. It gives me something to focus on in times of deep upheaval – and during this time, I was taking whatever I could get.

One of the biggest knots I was untangling was the uprooting of every identifier I had once leaned on. The ways I had labelled myself were suddenly no longer there.

I used to pride myself on being the 'six-figure business owner' – and now I couldn't even work one 45-minute session a week.

I thrived on my nine-hour sleeps – and now I'd be lucky to get two uninterrupted hours at a time.

I lived for my luxurious morning routines of journalling, card pulls and music – and now I didn't even want to write.

Every single minute piece of me fell away. Every point of joy I'd once held close. Every label I'd worn as a badge of honour. All of it burned away.

I wasn't the business owner anymore.

I wasn't making money anymore.

I wasn't a joyful, magnetic woman anymore.

I wasn't a healthy, vibrant, positive, glass-half-full woman anymore.

I wasn't a happy woman anymore.

It didn't make sense. I had the dream home. I had the healthy baby. I had the book deal. I had a beautiful, loving and hands-on husband supporting me.

And none of it mattered. None of it was enough.

Because I didn't know who I was anymore.

Because I didn't have me.

CHAPTER 2

Who Am I?

Take a moment to pull up your Instagram. If you don't use Instagram, then another social media platform that requires some form of bio is fine.

Go straight to your profile and have a read of the words listed under your name. Your bio. How do you describe yourself?

Are you someone who lists the names of your kids, or that of your partner, followed by a love heart emoji? (Cute!)

Are you more inclined to share your job title (or titles) and what you do in exchange for money?

Maybe you've listed your Sun, Moon and Rising, your human design profile or your favourite Bible verse?

Your bio tells me everything I need to know about how you see yourself – or perhaps, more importantly, how you want others to see you.

Now, imagine that whatever you have listed in your bio no longer exists (heavy, I know, but bear with me). What is left? Who are you when what you define yourself by is taken away?

This is where I found myself.

I had NFI who I was anymore, and no clue where to even start looking. It was like a giant life-size *Where's Hollie?* and I was the one I was looking for. Nothing made sense. Life as I knew it was over, which sounds dramatic, but is truly how I felt. I had no choice but to live anew. I could avoid the reality that was before me – that I could no longer live a happy, fulfilled life the way I was before my giant initiation – or I could walk straight into the flames and invite them to transmute and alchemise.

Obviously, your girl walked straight in.

The Australasian Birth Trauma Association describes matrescence as the physical, emotional, hormonal and social transition of becoming a mother.[1] Among a stifling array of physical, hormonal and emotional symptoms, new mothers can also experience feelings of loss of self, priority shifts and uncertainty about their abilities as a parent,[2] resulting in low confidence, self-esteem and, in my experience, a complete disconnect from our own inner knowing, self-trust and intuition.

If you know anything about me, you know that the biggest lesson I used to teach is intuition: how to live with it at the forefront of your days, how to tune in, how to listen to your heart among the noise of everyone outside of self. So you bet I was as surprised as anyone when I found myself rabbit-holing in late-night Google searches, new motherhood forums and social media Q&As in the first few months of my own matrescence.

I'd lost my intuition. The biggest part of me. The piece I'd leaned on in every major life moment to date. She was gone. And for the life of me, I didn't know how to get her back.

1 birthtrauma.org.au/what-is-matrescence
2 nayacare.org/blog/5-things-that-happen-with-matrescence

I decided to pick the brain of my wonderful friend Brittany Wilde, who has studied applied neuroscience and exercise science. Who even are we, when everything we have defined ourselves by falls away? And how do we start to pick up the pieces?

'Identity is a beast to understand, as it expresses itself as the combined sum total of experience, genetics, epigenetics, personal projects, culture, environment, relationships, exposures, biology, and natural idiosyncrasies,' she shared.

What this means is, contrary to popular belief (and pop culture), identity isn't some fixed thing that we are born with.

Britt describes identity as more movable than most believe. 'Identity evolves with each day, life season, personal experience, world event, personal project and spiritual transformation we live through. The simplest way to understand this is to think about who you were ten years ago, five years ago and even one year ago. How much has changed with the way you express yourself, what you enjoy doing, the kind of music you like, the standards you hold in your relationships, the dreams that you hold for your life?'

Which makes absolute sense in the context of becoming a mother. No longer was I the version of myself I was a year ago, or even a few months ago.

So the question is, rather than fight it (which I did for a long time), how can we embrace these unavoidable changes while avoiding a crisis? How can we become okay with not being the same person we once were?

'Identity isn't always a constant upward trajectory,' Britt shared. 'When we experience hardship – grief, loss, major change like having children or the endings of relationships – we can develop less pleasant expressions of our identity.'

Our very first sense of self forms in childhood or, in some psychological theories, even before we are born. Socioeconomic factors, environmental factors and other outside influences determined by the time we are conceived and then born (such as media, collective mainstream narratives and cultural privileges) all heavily influence how we naturally present to the world.

It's important that when we start exploring our personal identity, we look at where we have come from. Yep, our parents. And their parents. And theirs. This is the nitty-gritty and oftentimes painful part of a deconditioning process – that is, recognising what parts of your history you want to carry with you, and what parts you refuse to pull along as your truth.

I asked Britt to explain this in the context of epigenetics. She shared:

> Genetic biologist Professor Randy Jirtle says, 'Your genetic code can't be changed, but how it's read can. That's what epigenetics is all about.' What he's getting at is that your ancestors pass down imprints of their experiences – the good, the bad and the ugly – that can be stored in your body, and while you can't change your genes, you can change your gene expression based on how you think, move, act, eat, drink, respond and process. This expression is the subject of epigenetics.
>
> So, while you are not the sum total of your parents and their experiences, they most certainly play a role in your life. The beautiful news is that you can change what you

can see. Through the process of exploring the major life milestones, moments and core themes of the lives of your ancestors, you can bring to your awareness the epigenetic hand-me-downs you've inherited. Then, you can decide what you're going to do about it. Awareness precedes all action, so by shining a light on what was, you can act on what you wish to be by putting yourself in environments, relationships, challenges, hobbies and internal states that cultivate healthy expressions of your genes.

ACTIVITY: **Where did you come from?**

Before we look at who you are today, we need to look at where you've come from. This gives us a clear understanding of the conditioning that occurred for you way before you were even born. The stuff that you couldn't help then, but perhaps you can now.

Take a moment to write down everything you know about your parents' identities before you were born. Think about the families they were born into. What was growing up like for them? How did they live? What was their social status? Were they accepted or 'different'? What was home life like?

Write until you have a clear understanding of some of the key throughlines of their experiences.

For example, my father is from a migrant family. This tells me so much about how his identity would have been formed from as early as a newborn. They were the 'wogs', the different ones, the poor ones. My dad shares stories about how his family couldn't afford shoes when he was a child. These are the key points of identity formation we are looking for. Because whether this is our own experience or not, we carry these imprints with us. But once we are aware, we can choose which of these we *want* to carry, and which we want to walk away from.

By the time we reach adolescence, our identity is well and truly starting to form. According to Erik Erikson's theory of psychosocial development, our identity formation meets eight Stages of Development – from newborn life until well into late adulthood.[3] According to Erikson, we first begin to establish and experiment with our sense of identity from the ages of 12–18. He coins this time of adolescence as our first real 'identity crisis' – when we start to experiment with who we are, what we believe and how that has us sit among our peers, family and society as a whole. In fact, Erikson believes the primary psychosocial focus of adolescence is establishing our identity.[4]

In layman's terms? Our teenage years are some of the most hectic, intense, soul-disruptive, ego-dying years of our lives. But rather than offering deep reverence, respect and safe space-holding for the psychological upheaval this time brings, modern-day culture has dismissed this rite of passage with

3 courses.lumenlearning.com/adolescent/chapter/identity-development-theory
4 courses.lumenlearning.com/adolescent/chapter/identity-development-theory

an eye roll, and infused it with criticism, judgement and stereotyping. It's like a giant societal gaslighting, where what we experience as teenagers is very real and very normal, but we are left questioning if we are the only ones, and are we actually going crazy?

What would our teenage years have been like if, rather than being seen as hormonal, emotional, disruptive troublemakers, we'd had the space to openly and vulnerably share the confusion and challenge of that time while we were navigating it? How would our experience of who we are, and the depth of our identity formation, have been different? Imagine if rather than it coming as a shock, and as a period of intense isolation and deep-seated emotional upheaval, we were offered safe spaces to process, to heal, to share and to burn. To rise again. What would life be like if our truth and vulnerability were tended to at such a deeply fragile and formative time?

What would life be like if we were to honour not just this, but all rites of passage?

I truly believe that if our first rite of passage was honoured in a whole new way, then perhaps we would have fewer adults avoiding feeling deeply, and with less fear, when it came to times of deep repatterning, reconditioning and ego upheaval.

Factors like childhood trauma have an impact on identity development in adolescence, and beyond, and can cause identity diffusion, which is defined as the 'loss of capacity for self-definition and commitment to values, goals, or relationships and a painful sense of incoherence'.[5] On the other hand, when our identity is integrated, we can have more confidence, greater self-esteem and feel that life has deeper meaning.[6]

5 www.sciencedirect.com/science/article/abs/pii/S0140197119301320
6 www.sciencedirect.com/science/article/abs/pii/S0140197119301320

Teenagers who have stable upbringings are likely to also experience a more stable exploration of their identity as a result – like a trial and error of sorts, with friendships, hobbies, appearance, sexuality and the list goes on. From this place, their identities can integrate in a more solid way.

My teenage years were equal parts some of the best and the worst of my life. I loved school and excelled because I worked hard. But I also spent them constantly on guard, feeling unsafe because of trauma I had experienced as a child.

Someone experiencing adolescence the way I did is more likely to have been susceptible to identity diffusion. That means that, due to the traumas of their upbringing, they are more likely to experience negative expectations of self or the future, self-blame, feelings of detachment, diminished interest in previously enjoyed activities, and/or major disruptions in a social context – all of which can negatively impact identity formation.[7]

While this may not manifest immediately, it can become all too apparent when triggered later in life – like when I lost all sense of who I was in my huge rite of passage and initiation into motherhood.

All of a sudden, the things I loved no longer interested me, I felt completely isolated from my friends and family; I didn't see any positivity in my future (I had exceptionally dark thoughts at this time, thinking that my life was genuinely over) and felt completely detached from my experiences.

If I knew at the time that what I was experiencing was identity diffusion as a result of my traumatic upbringing, perhaps things

7 www.sciencedirect.com/science/article/abs/pii/S0140197119301320

would have made a little more sense. Perhaps I could have created spaces that felt safe to process. Instead, as the saying goes, before it got better, it had to get worse.

CHAPTER 3

The Hardest Part

My first two years of motherhood read like a really farfetched teen drama from the early noughties. (I'm feeling *One Tree Hill* vibes. If you agree, you have excellent taste in television.)

Even though I'm not writing a TV drama, it's important to highlight the multiple moving parts that I was navigating during my big identity collapse. It wasn't only matrescence; the string of complexities of those two years are enough to make anyone shake their head in disbelief.

For the sake of brevity, I'll list them as a timeline.

December 2021

My daughter was a posterior baby born via episiotomy and forceps delivery during mandatory Covid restrictions, following a marathon 47-hour active labour, the majority of which I declined pain relief for, and then spent the entirety of it projectile vomiting from the pain. The pressure I had placed on myself, and what it meant to be a mother who birthed without intervention and as naturally as possible, was the first part of my identity that had to die.

January 2022

The months following her birth saw undetected low milk supply, meaning she didn't gain any weight for three months – in fact, she lost 900 grams that first week – and yet none of the private midwives told me anything was wrong. I was watching my daughter fade away in front of me with no one telling me what to do.

It was like a horror movie. My ability to trust in professionals, receive help and listen to my intuition all crumbled. I was outsourcing every inkling I had, to no avail. Things were getting worse. My identity as an intuitive person completely fell away.

February 2022

My low milk supply sent me into a spiral which, at its worst, saw me piercing my nipples with sterile needles multiple times a day to try to clear the blocked milk. I would pump for an hour and be lucky to get 10mls of milk. You name it, I did it. I refused to 'give up' and was gladly breaking myself down rather than contemplating a new motherhood journey that did not include breastfeeding. I had mastitis constantly, was on antibiotics to fight the fevers and pain and was stuck to the couch for marathon feeding sessions I thought were cluster feeds, but was later told was just my little girl trying to get every tiny drop from me (18 hours at a time). I used nipple shields, a supply line and other women's breastmilk to try to bring on my own. I took tonics and tinctures, had scans and ultrasounds and cried many, many, many tears of guttural grief.

My mental health was severely declining because I had attached myself to the identity of 'breastfeeding mother', and what did it mean if I couldn't be one? I was terrified of what people would think of me if I bottle-fed in public (even though I couldn't breastfeed at home, let alone in public). The alternative? Never leave the house. I was isolating myself because I was so afraid of what other people might say, when my internal dialogue was the worst of them all.

At the same time, our region experienced one of its most severe floods in history. While our own home was safe, we had no safe means to leave with our three-month-old, and all of the grocery stores in our small town were emptied out, meaning there was no formula for our little girl. One night, we had completely run out of formula and my milk had all but dried up. If it wasn't for mothers in another state shipping their donor breastmilk down to us, I wouldn't have had a way to feed my baby.

I didn't feel safe to be a mother. It wasn't safe. I could no longer trust in life.

March 2022

One of our dearest friends was in a tragic accident that left him in a coma. For five weeks, we woke every morning waiting to hear the news of if he had woken up, or died. While he survived – and his story is not mine to tell – the impact of a loved one in such a traumatic place compounded the traumas we were already experiencing as a family.

August 2022 – August 2023

I was in and out of therapy sessions, blood tests, scans and alternative health consultations for a full year, trying to uncover the root cause of my physical pain and inflammation. I was diagnosed with postnatal depression, complex PTSD, compound trauma and a multitude of physical manifestations, including hypertonic pelvic floor, hypothyroidism, adrenal fatigue and chronic inflammation, which has since led to a recent mast cell activation syndrome (MCAS) diagnosis.

My mental health was at its lowest. I was doing all I could via various therapeutic modalities to shift my mental state, while my physical body was inflamed, swollen and finding it hard to get through the day without completely breaking at the seams. I left my own birthday dinner before anyone else because my eyes had started to swell shut, as a result of the chronic inflammation. I spent every day in physical pain, unable to recognise myself, while still having to show up for my business.

While navigating all of the above, I was needing to show up for my little girl as her primary care giver, 24/7. She was my priority – as our children are – above and beyond myself. On reflection, I actually don't know how I did it.

November 2023

On the precipice of my daughter's second birthday, we had to evacuate our home by police order because our neighbour had been stockpiling guns and explosives and was threatening to set them off. This happened 100 metres from our front door.

Now, add to the above the more standard, everyday stressors of being a new mother. The endless washing (sans dishwasher in our case #churchhousethings). The car-averse daughter who would vomit on trips more than 15 minutes from home. The lack of family nearby for support, so a constant tag-teaming between me and Trent as we both tried to adapt to this new life rhythm. A business that saw two failed launches within six months of 'coming back' to work (that is, no one purchasing a thing from me. Not one thing). Financial stressors of being a homeowner and sole trader in a doleful economic climate.

Life continued life-ing, even in the shitstorm of traumatic events, and there was no other option but to put one foot in front of the other. There were many days – hundreds of them, in fact – where I didn't even leave the house for the enormity of it all.

And you know what? Even among all of that – so much stress, hypervigilance, initiation and strength demanded of me – none of that was the worst thing that happened in those two years. Not even close.

The worst thing that happened was cutting my dad out of my life.

I feel sick even writing these words, because it makes it real.

Most people in my life have been incredibly supportive of this decision, but the truth is that even in choosing to saying yes to me in such a bold way, a part of me – the daughter in me, the little girl in me, the part of me that, despite all of it, still loves him – still wants to protect him. To protect my family. To wear a mask, like the 13-year-old in me writing poetry, who says it's all okay. The thing is … it isn't. And it hasn't been for a very long time.

And without airing any dirty laundry, I will say this:

Any person – no matter the role they play in your life – who continually disrespects, oversteps and downright abuses the boundaries you set in your own life is not deserving of occupying any space in it.

That is the cold, hard truth.

Now, I don't need to justify my boundaries to anyone, but for the sake of context, I don't ask for much, just that I expect to be treated with kindness and considered communication, as I treat those in my life. That said, my initiation into motherhood has ignited in me a steadfast will to model behaviours for my little girl, so she will never question holding her own boundaries, not for a second. And to be that role model for her, I have to model that behaviour. I need to process my own trauma to ensure she won't receive that same inheritance.

This decision did not happen overnight. I have spent decades in therapy, unpacking my deep-seated trauma as well as my relationship with my parents. While my mum and I have had many challenging yet healing conversations, I have not experienced the same with my dad. In fact, things were getting worse. And while I was navigating the above traumatic timeline, I realised that I didn't need to carry that additional burden anymore. There was only so much I could do, before I decided I couldn't possibly do any more.

It wasn't as simple as taking off a heavy backpack and placing it on the ground, walking away lighter. This was the hardest decision I have ever made in my life. One I still question every day. It's in a child's biological makeup to choose their parents.

But when faced with this kind of decision, the biggest move is to choose yourself, even when it comes at a cost of biological drives.

So when I talk about doing the work it takes to really, truly choose you, please know that I'm not just talking from a pile of Instagrammable buzzwords. I'm talking from raw and lived experience. I'm talking from navigating parts that are not yet complete. I am speaking not from a place of being healed, but of being fully committed to my healing. That is the real difference. I'm not standing on a pedestal, declaring, 'This is how it should be done.' I'm sitting on the couch next to you, our cacaos spiked with Reishi (for our overactive stress hormones), having a heart to heart. More questions than answers. More crumblings than completions.

But also more open-hearted than I have ever been. Because I am willingly taking off the masks that have had me hidden for so long. I don't want to hide anymore.

And I know that you don't either.

SECTION 2

Slow Down, Tune In and Shine Bright

CHAPTER 4

Back to Basics

The only reason I can openly write everything I have shared so far is that – believe it or not – I am writing from a place of aligned truth. While the last two years have been some of the most challenging of my life so far, they have also been my greatest life initiators. I can confidently say I am the best version of myself, in every way, because of the past two years. Turns out, our identity is formed as much in the tumultuous moments as the shiny ones.

Today, I can honestly say I love motherhood with all my heart, which, just over a year ago, I didn't know I would ever say. My little girl is the highlight of my day, and I spend most of my time in full body giggles with her as a proud stay-at-home mum. I have recently signed a contract with new modelling management while being lead understudy for a local award-winning theatre company. We are off on our first family overseas holiday once I hand my draft version of this book into my publisher. My relationship with my husband is slowly but surely back on track after two years of tag-teaming as roommates more than lovers (you try having a libido in a two-year-long shitstorm!). We're planning to move closer to the coast, to tend to the quality of life we desire now that we are out of the trenches of new parenthood.

Once again, life is full, in the most incredibly inspiring, uplifting and magical ways. Such are its ebbs and flows. And while the last two years took me out, I also surrendered to their teachings, listened to their whispers and am now building myself back up to a shinier place than I've ever been.

And I mean it when I say that I never thought I'd see these moments when I was in the depths of my identity collapse. Life was about surviving. Getting through each moment, remembering to breathe, sleep, eat. Everything was stripped back to basics. My physical body was crying out for help and, to be honest, it still is. Chronic stress and inflammation, as well as recovering from complex PTSD and decades of trauma, all require a slow and intentional unravelling to re-establish (or, if you're anything like me, actually establish for the first time in your adult life) a solid baseline.

I have 30 years of trauma to decompress, and it's taken me some time to realise this isn't just going to shift after a few therapy sessions. No – healing takes time.

But the beauty of it all being stripped back to basics in those first years of postpartum was that I had a clean slate. I got to say yes to my life once more, in entirely new ways, because I was an entirely new person.

And it all started with slowing things down.

When it comes to truly saying yes to you, you must say yes to the full spectrum of your story. To slow down, tune in and shine bright requires a level of radical self-honesty which forms the basis of authentic living, an acceptance that perhaps there is more work to be done than ideal and a resistance to seeking a quick fix. These days we're so used to the next 'magic pill', or jumping on a juice detox, a weekend retreat, a women's circle, seeking something – anything – to heal us quickly. The truth is this level of healing takes time. And it isn't often an enjoyable process. It's messy and it's confronting. It's hard work.

Every time I try to turn a blind eye to my trauma, what I'm actually doing is dismissing the biggest piece of me that wants to be looked at. In brushing away the confronting truths, I'm choosing to avoid the healing. To avoid the 'hard'.

This week I received blood test results highlighting a decline in health markers connected to my thyroid. As someone with a history of autoimmune conditions (psoriasis and hypothyroidism), as well as a sister who lives with type 1 diabetes that wasn't diagnosed until her twenties, I am fully aware of the erratic nature of autoimmune conditions, and the toll that living with a chronic illness takes. Just when you think you're on top of your health, it takes a dive. Such is the nature of any illness that is largely caused by stress.

In my meditation this morning, as I was contemplating this decline in my physical health, I started to join the (somewhat apparent) dots between the people I know in my life with a chronic illness and their experiences of childhood trauma. There was a strong correlation, enough to make me dive into the plethora of research online, where I found that there is strong evidence that if you grow up in an abusive home environment, you are more likely to develop chronic illness and autoimmune conditions than someone who did not.

One study documents a consistent association between childhood trauma and negative health consequences in adulthood (including stress-related illnesses, suppressed immune functioning and unexplained somatic symptoms).[8]

Another study found that adults with a higher ACE score (Adverse Childhood Experiences like abuse, neglect, household violence, addiction etc.) are also at higher risk of autoimmune conditions, evidencing that exposure to 'traumatic toxic stress' triggers changes in the immune system.[9]

Add to the above that children who have grown up with a multitude of ACEs are likely operating from a baseline of PTSD well into adulthood.[10] Because of this heightened stress response being switched on and active over decades, the stress in the body can culminate into autoimmune and/or neurological conditions. While there is no clear single cause for these chronic illnesses, research is increasingly highlighting ACEs as a prominent piece of the puzzle.

This is why trauma-informed care is so important. Because, for someone like me – who pushed herself through a 47-hour posterior labour in the name of 'high pain threshold' (read: traumatised nervous system) – that then had a cascading negative effect on my low oxytocin levels, stifled my milk production and tipped me over into complex PTSD. What probably looked like a case of another birth plan going awry was in fact a highly traumatised woman trying to 'push through' her trauma based on what she thought was possible because of what she'd seen reflected externally. The other

8 www.ncbi.nlm.nih.gov/pmc/articles/PMC3153850
9 www.healthline.com/health/chronic-illness/childhood-trauma-connected-chronic-illness#A-closer-look-at-ACEs
10 www.healthline.com/health/chronic-illness/childhood-trauma-connected-chronic-illness#A-closer-look-at-ACEs

natural-birthing mothers online. The private midwives telling her that, given all of the 'prep work' she had done for birth, she could do it.

Guess what? For my deeply traumatised, painfully constricted and inflamed body, it simply wasn't possible. But because there was no trauma-informed care on hand, I wonder if anyone guessed that what was playing out during my little girl's birth was in fact my own amplified trauma response?

That's the thing with chronic stress, chronic illness and any sort of invisible health condition. It is such an entrenched part of our identity that it goes unrecognised by most people who have not had a similar experience. And that is understandable because, from the outside looking in, many of us seem to be thriving, because we've never been given any other option than to keep going. To do it all, as if we were normal, functioning healthy adults. Because what choice do we have? We still have our children to care for, we still have money that needs to be made, mortgages to pay for, creative outlets that bring us joy.

The difference is that we've adapted. We know how to do it, consistently running on empty – and with little recognition for just how hard it is – all the time. We get by.

How hard it is for us to live, let alone thrive.

The unfair irony of this all is it is just such a mirror to my childhood, and likely the childhood of many people with a chronic illness. We wear a mask. We don't let people see what's actually going on beneath the surface. That we're hurting. Before the traumas became physical, I was navigating life by just getting by as best I could. Whacking a smile on my face, working overtime, studying hard, keeping myself busy …

And now, although navigating an entirely different set of painful circumstances, I catch myself resorting back to that same comfortable mask. The difference now that my physical body is crying out for recognition and slowing down is that I'm taking the mask off.

I'm tired of pretending.

> **nervous system**[11] / noun
> the bodily system that in vertebrates is made up of the brain and spinal cord, nerves, ganglia, and parts of the receptor organs and that receives and interprets stimuli and transmits impulses to the effector organs
>
> **regulate**[12] / verb
> to control something, especially by making it work in a particular way

In this day and age, are you even working in personal development if you don't talk about the nervous system and how to regulate it?

Jokes aside, to really grasp the nature of slowing down and its impact on choosing ourselves, it's important that we develop a solid understanding of what our nervous system actually is, and proven ways to *actually* regulate it, versus what the latest Wim Hof superfan claims online.

11 www.merriam-webster.com/dictionary/nervous%20system
12 dictionary.cambridge.org/dictionary/english/regulate

Social media is wonderful for so many reasons. Heck, I likely wouldn't be writing my books without it. I adore it for connection, having made many of my dearest friends online, and my business has thrived off the back of the wonderful community of clients, readers and 'followers' I have connected with over the years (hi guys!). The challenge of social media is everyone appears to be an 'expert' at whatever it is they hold an opinion about. When it comes to our relationship with our health and wellbeing, that can do far more harm than good.

One of the biggest buzzwords or, more accurately, 'buzz phrases' I'm seeing currently is that of 'nervous system regulation'. Where one coach speaks about the benefits of hot and cold therapy, another speaks about the harm. Where one motivational speaker talks about the power of breathwork, another highlights nutrition as the most important foundation. Use blue-light blockers. Don't scroll before bed. Meditate. Journal. Eat meat. Don't eat meat. Drink coffee. Don't drink coffee. Take adaptogenic mushrooms. Detox your cleaning products.

The list never ends. And, to be totally transparent, I have added my voice and opinion to many of these. I used to work in the beauty industry advocating how important switching to natural beauty products is for our hormones and overall wellbeing. I use a water filter. I walk barefoot most places. I take my turmeric capsules every day. I wear a Whoop, for godsake. I am absolutely not denying my role in this wellness influencer cliche.

What I'm grappling with currently, in my own journey of claiming a stable nervous system (something I have honestly never experienced in my entire life), is what true regulation of our nervous system is, as opposed to what is a regurgitated tick-box of stress relievers or wellness-enhancing hacks. What makes for a good Insta-reel aesthetic does not always have the knowledge and depth required to provide deep and proven tools for solid regulation. So, I reached out to one of the only voices on social media right now I trust when it comes to commentary on nervous system regulation.

Dr Scherina Alli is a network spinal doctor who has amassed an impressive online community of more than 395,000 people across the world tuning in to her considered, informed and peaceful approach to nervous system healing.

I asked her how she would describe nervous system regulation. She shared:

> One word – adaptability. Nervous system regulation does not mean you are calm all of the time. That's just unrealistic in today's world. Nervous system regulation means that we've created resilience within to enable our nervous system to adapt to the daily stressors we may encounter without being sent into a downward spiral or development of unhealthy protective patterns.
>
> Every person is in a different place – some people can jump right into cathartic emotional releases and some will be set off into panic attacks for weeks. If you're working with someone, or a practice to help bring you into regulation, make sure they are doing a proper assessment of your current nervous system state.

This is especially important to recognise for those of us who are living with any form of traumatic or chronic stress or mood disorder, as well as any autoimmune conditions. Because every single one of our systems is unique, there are very few things that will work across the board for all of us, all of the time. Our unique life experiences, and exactly what we are deconditioning from, are going to determine what our bodies – and nervous systems – need to thrive in any given moment. For each of us, that will look radically different, and finding the methods that work best for you is often a matter of trial and error.

For example, while I love a hot bath or sweat sesh in a sauna, I've noticed that extreme heat does not currently serve me when it comes to my baseline recovery. In fact, it puts my system into a high stress response, which I currently do not have the window of tolerance to hold or process like the average healthy person, so I end up feeling worse. So even though yes, bubble baths and sauna times are wonderful methods of decompression and relaxation for many of us, for just as many of us, they are our poison.

This is where nuance cannot be overlooked in conversations around nervous system regulation. There is a very real difference between self-care practices for stress management and nervous system measures to cultivate a deep rest response in someone whose nervous system is operating at the bare minimum.

This is me. And it's also anyone who has experienced, or is currently moving through, PTSD, chronic stress and/or any inflammatory or autoimmune condition. I would go so far to say that it also goes for anyone navigating a total identity crumble. Because in the crumbling, there is only so much our system's window of tolerance can hold.

What *actually* serves us are measures that slow us down, on all fronts. Space. Rest. The breath. This is where regulation actually happens. And this is what we are most likely to resist, because our bodies feel more familiar – and therefore 'safer' – when we are functioning on adrenaline and running ourselves into the ground.

We all know the fight-and-flight response, that back in caveman days we were wired to react quickly to any imposing, life-threatening danger (like a sabre-toothed tiger approaching) and our bodies instantly pushed us to fight or run away to safety – or perhaps freeze or fawn. This is an in-built biological response to keep us safe. To keep us alive.

When someone has experienced decades of trauma, abuse and/or physical illness, they are far more inclined to be operating from one of these responses as a baseline, all of the time, no matter the intensity of the incoming 'stressor'. Emails. Texts that need a reply. That FaceTime with your friend later today. A back-to-back day as a stay-at-home mum, where the stressors literally DO NOT STOP from the second you open your eyes (am I right?).

So while there isn't any sabre-toothed tiger coming for us, it absolutely *feels* like there is. For me, especially after we were evacuated from our home last year, I often lie awake at night, waiting to hear any sound that could be classified as 'danger'. I am in a whole new world of hypervigilance, and a bubble bath or sauna at the end of the day is absolutely not enough to help me out of it.

As Dr Scherina shared, 'We have to start to listen to our body! This means paying attention to how we feel when we encounter stress, when we come face to face with conflict, when we're triggered. What is our body telling us – do we feel panic?

Do we shut down? Are we reactive? Do we become aggressive? All very important emotions to feel so we can re-learn our body.'

I was never going to be one of 'those wellness people' who wore a biometric tracker. To be honest, I didn't take much interest in products like the Whoop, or the Oura ring (biometric tracking devices worn to collate and share your personalised health and recovery markers). They were for the athletes, or at least the people who trained regularly. And just to be very clear, I am neither of the above.

It wasn't until I purchased a Whoop for Trent for Christmas – following the strong recommendation from my friend Britt – that I started to notice how valuable this awareness of health data could be for someone like me. I started to become curious about sleep quality and depth, what created high stress levels in me versus someone else, and that ever-elusive HRV (heart rate variability). Within three weeks of Trent wearing his, I had purchased my own. And not because I was all of a sudden going to start training for a marathon. I just wanted to get an understanding of my baseline nervous system.

What WAS making me stressed? How was my HRV performing?

It's important to note this lingo was all very new to me. If you mentioned HRV to me even six months ago, I'd think you were talking about a type of car. I was genuinely none the wiser and hadn't expected to look at any data because 'that's not who I am'. I trust my body and listen to her cues; I don't need a tracker to tell me when I'm stressed.

But what this data illuminated for me is that my nervous system baseline was actually far lower than I had anticipated.

While, yes, the fog of postpartum days had lifted and so – comparatively speaking – I felt much better than I had the previous couple of years, my markers were all showing signs of heightened stress levels, chronic inflammation and PTSD.

My HRV on a very good day (at the time of writing) sits at 29/30 (as a comparison, my relatively untraumatised husband sits at an average of 110).

My resting heart rate (RHR) sits between 75–80 bpm (again, chill husband sits at around 55).

It's been three solid months of tracking this data and quantifying what my body is telling me. And while I feel better than I have in a long time, my body is still fighting chronic stress, inflammation and trauma. I was in denial about how bad my heath actually was until I saw the data.

According to Whoop, HRV is a measure of time between heartbeats, and is an indicator of the body's autonomic nervous system, which is made up of the sympathetic and parasympathetic systems.[13] The sympathetic response is what I refer to above, when talking about fight-or-flight. For someone like me, this is easy to access; I'm there all the time. I'm great in a crisis because my system is constantly on high alert. I've called emergency services in moments of crisis more times than I can count – when a colleague passed out in my arms after donating blood, when my teacher at school had a heart attack in front of the class (I actually ran away on that occasion – cue 'flight' response – but to get help, no less), when I was one of the first on the scene of a car accident. The sympathetic response is what has us jumping into action. And anyone who has experienced

13 www.whoop.com/au/en/thelocker/low-hrv

trauma or abuse will likely understand it when I say that it feels like this is just a baseline operating system.

The parasympathetic nervous system, on the other hand, is responsible for what is known as 'rest and digest'. Pretty self-explanatory, right? If only it were as simple to embody. I struggle to even enter this state. My body thrives in a sympathetic response because of the 30-plus years I've had to stay on my toes for safety's sake. To literally keep safe, I've had to constantly be scanning my environments for 'danger'. My body also has NFI what it actually means to rest and digest. This is the response that lowers heart rate, blood pressure and respiration rate, and supports digestion.[14] To be a healthy functioning human with a regulated nervous system, we require both systems.

This is why HRV tracking is such a game-changer. Because in only three months of tracking my own, it has become very clear that my parasympathetic nervous system needs some love. Actually, scrap that – it needs a complete overhaul.

My life needs a complete overhaul.

My hopes for really homing in on this area of my life? That I will start to actually feel well again. That eventually I'll be able to get through the day without the need for a nap, or without waking three times a night. That I'll have more energy to give my growing little family. That my first response to any given situation won't be that of panic or stress. That I'll walk slower, breathe deeper and smile wider. This overhaul isn't just about an increase in metrics. It's about an increase in my capacity to live a full, beautiful and thriving life on my own terms – without being dictated to by what has happened to me in the past.

14 www.whoop.com/au/en/thelocker/low-hrv

So, how do we do this?

Well – lucky for you – I am using myself as a crash-test dummy. I have been trialling a multitude of practices, all with solid backing from experts I fully trust, to see what has a significant impact on my HRV, and therefore my parasympathetic state. I have enlisted additional support to nourish my baseline nervous system from the ground up, all the while tracking the solid data of my nervous system on my Whoop.

Remember – working on our own nervous system is a nuanced and tailored journey. It's highly dependent on a multitude of factors that make up the unique life story that is yours, and yours alone. When hearing from these experts and walking you through these practices, my objective is to highlight the practices that can benefit ALL of us – no matter our life path. These are our overall foundational practices for a solid baseline nervous system. These are our starting point, before we rush off into anything complex or a popular trend we've seen online.

Britt is the first practitioner I sat down with to gauge an understanding of where to even begin when it came to regulating my nervous system (read: slowing things the fuck down). Because it's one thing to know that something needs to change (in my case, a whole lot!) – but another thing entirely to cut through the noise and, quite frankly, BS online and actually get to the core of what is impactful, result-focused, trauma-informed and also – in my case – relatively easy to implement as a nonstop stay-at-home mum of a two-year-old who is also writing a book and appearing in a play (living the dream).

In my appointment with Britt, we sat down and reviewed my biometric data (including my HRV, RHR and stress and sleep metrics) alongside her deep awareness of all I have navigated in recent years (Britt was a solid rock for me in postpartum, even donating her own breastmilk for my little girl). We came up with a relatively quick and simple actionable plan to work on right away.

This looked like:

Adequate hydration

Not just in quantity, but quality (filtered water with added electrolytes).

I asked Britt why hydration was at the top of the list when it came to addressing my baseline nervous system metrics. She shared, 'Most people wildly misunderstand hydration, and conflate it with water intake. So, while water volume obviously matters and needs to meet your body's physiological needs, what matters more is the quality of the water and electrolyte balance. To maintain optimal function, the balance of electrolytes such as sodium, potassium and magnesium are vital. Water quality is also paramount, as many water systems contain chlorine and copper as a result of corrosion in copper pipes. Filtered water with added electrolytes creates one of the biggest marked improvements in recovery scores and HRV measurements than any other variable.'

Morning sunlight

Ideally within the first 30 minutes of waking.

Britt shares, 'Getting even five to ten minutes of early morning sun exposure can dramatically improve health. It regulates your circadian rhythm – responsible for alertness and sleep readiness – which is predominantly driven by dark and light cycles. When you get sunlight on your skin, you trigger the suppression of melatonin (the sleep hormone) throughout the day so you're alert and ready to tackle life, and it sets in motion a body "alarm" that will go off 12–16 hours after first light exposure, releasing melatonin for sleep readiness. Not only does it regulate sleep and wake cycles, it also stimulates the production of serotonin, a neurotransmitter associated with mood regulation and feelings of wellbeing. Finally, sunlight exposure is essential for the synthesis of vitamin D in the skin, which plays a crucial role in bone health and immune function. It's one of the easiest habits to implement to create a significant improvement in energy throughout the day and quality of sleep at night.'

A solid sleep regime

With a focus on consistency (keeping awake and sleep windows within 30 minutes of one another) and environment (white noise, blackout blinds and a cosy environment. And, yes, that means no screens in bed!).

We really started with the basics – water, sun and sleep.

Rather than adding anything overwhelming to my already-overwhelmed system, it was important to start by introducing relatively simple, easy changes that actually – over time – can see a profound shift in parasympathetic states.

I also enlisted the help of functional medicine practitioner Chantel Hutnan to review my latest blood work and overall health markers. Based on a number of autoimmune markers that were increasing from my last set of bloodwork, as well as an indication of depleted adrenals and a slow-working liver (all a result of accumulated chronic stress spanning decades), she wanted me to focus on entering the parasympathetic state as often as possible through nutrition and supplementation.

To do this, her guidance included well-rounded meals at regular intervals throughout the day. My lack of snacking, and six hours between meals, was no longer going to cut it.

I asked Chantel to explain why stabilising our blood sugar levels is paramount to a supported nervous system, and often one of the first steps she looks at in clients who are struggling to access the parasympathetic nervous system.

She shared, 'The reason stabilising our blood sugar levels is so important is that spikes in blood glucose from dietary inputs often result in blood glucose dips or reactive hypoglycaemia. Your body is genetically programmed to recognise low blood sugar as a threat to survival. The immediate response to bring blood glucose back up happens through activation of the sympathetic nervous system to release adrenaline and cortisol. This can perpetuate a cycle of constant "stress" response activation.'

So the introduction of regular carbohydrates and consistent mealtimes is so much more than sound nutrition. It is communicating to my body that it is safe, that there is adequate food available to it and it doesn't have to spike my glucose levels from a place of stress when more hours go by without food.

In only a week of introducing this new approach, my RHR dropped seven per cent. In two weeks, my HRV increased ten points above my standard maximum range.

We're onto something here.

ACTIVITY: **Simple nutritional practices to regulate your nervous system**

Let's take it right back to the basics. Block out all of that online noise and take a moment to scan over the following list of easy-to-execute nutritional practices that can all have a positive impact on your nervous system. These are practices supported from a functional medicine standpoint that I have also personally experienced results from implementing. When looking for your starting point, this is it.

- Eat within 30 minutes of waking up.
- Have your food before coffee.
- Each meal should contain adequate protein, fat and fibre to stabilise blood sugar and feed the beneficial gut microbes.

- Stick to an overnight 10–12 hour fast, maximum.
- Aim to consume food every three to four hours. Chantel shares that, 'While intermittent fasting and avoiding snacking are often effective for high blood sugar, eating more regularly throughout the day tends to work better for those with low blood sugar. This is often the case in hypothalamic pituitary adrenal dysfunction as a result of long-term activation of your stress response system.'
- Replenish key nutrients which are often more taxed – magnesium, B vitamins, vitamin C, sodium, potassium, zinc. (Find a health practitioner to support you with supplementation and blood test analysis.)
- Adaptogens like ashwagandha, rhodiola, schisandra, eleuthero and cordyceps are botanicals which increase resistance to physical or psychological stress, have a nonspecific immune-modulating effect and increase energy. If you're taking any prescribed medications, consult your healthcare professional before introducing any of these.

The irony of this specific shift in nutrition for me is that up until I became a mother, one of my biggest identifiers was that I was a pescetarian. For 17 years, in fact, I didn't eat any red or white meat, aside from seafood. This was a decision I 'randomly' made one day when I was 16, and never considered for a moment in those 17 years that I would ever eat meat again. It was such an intrinsic part of who I was. I wore it as a badge of honour.

While I absolutely pass no judgement on how you choose to fuel your body (you know your body more than I do!), I realise now that this way of nourishment was causing me far more harm than good. For 17 years, I was lacking the adequate protein intake for a traumatised body that was already struggling to operate at baseline nervous system stability. I'm not someone who thrives eating this way. But I'm nothing if not resilient and dismissed the physical factors pointing to an undernourished body. It became so deeply entrenched in my identity – especially as it was a mask I chose to put on in adolescence, during my first experience of identity diffusion – that I couldn't actually comprehend who I was without it. It was so much more than a certain way of eating; it was who I was. And when something is so deeply entrenched in who you are, recognising that it may be doing more harm than good is a very difficult wake-up call.

This way of eating was something I could control when life felt so out of my control. It made me feel like I was a good person. When I didn't eat meat, I felt superior – that's the truth of it. I felt like I knew more when, ironically, I knew far less. I felt morally on purpose (I am a huge animal lover), and smug, even as this way of living came at a cost to my physical wellbeing.

It wasn't until my next identity crisis in new motherhood that I realised this mask was not one I could continue to wear if I wanted to truly say yes to my life. If I wanted to really get my health on track, truly recover from pregnancy and birth, and recuperate from decades of trauma, my body needed to feel nourished, and safe. Like Chantel shares, each meal we eat should contain adequate protein, fat and fibre to stabilise blood sugar and feed the beneficial gut microbes. And, dare I say it, for 17 years, I was not consuming adequate protein. Not by a long shot.

I realised last year that my body requires animal products to function. For you, maybe it doesn't. I had to really look at myself and the identity story I had placed on this way of eating to recognise that this wasn't who I wanted to be. I chose my aligned health. And that meant choosing to eat meat again.

And that's the kind of gritty decision-making that happens when you're choosing you.

ACTIVITY: **Take off the mask**

Maybe you have a challenged relationship with the way you eat. And that is understandable – food and nourishment is so often charged because of its enmeshment with our emotional state of wellbeing.

As Chantel shares, 'Because of the complexity that comes with trauma, our attitudes and behaviours about food, eating and how we associate with food, our own self-image, how we manage stress and the dopamine responses to impulsive actions have a huge effect on what we put into our body, our physiology and our nervous system.'

I am not asking you to change the way you eat overnight, particularly if you experience disordered eating or body dysmorphia, in which case, I really hope you have found a practitioner to help you. This is not something to do alone.

This exercise is simply an opportunity to reflect. Perhaps even pull out your journal and start to ask yourself some questions. If you eat a certain way – under a certain label (vegan, vegetarian, pescetarian, ancestral, keto etc.) – why? When did you make this decision? How could this decision be a reflection of the period of life you were traversing at the time? Is it a decision that has considered your physical and mental health at the forefront? And, most importantly, is this way of eating truly nourishing you? The 'you' beneath all labels, judgements and masks?

Perhaps for you, this contemplation isn't about the way you eat. Maybe it's the way you drink. My dear friend Cass recently had her own experience of reflecting on her relationship with alcohol. She realised that for a large portion of her life, her identity as the 'fun party girl' was so enmeshed with binge drinking and abusing substances. In her journey into motherhood, experiencing her own identity collapse, she realised this was no longer a mask she wanted to wear. She decided to take off the party girl mask and step into sobriety.

At the time of writing, she has been six months sober, and has never felt more herself.

Four months have gone by since I have introduced these simple practices. And I do not say this lightly – they have changed my life significantly. For me, the biggest takeaway has been around how little I was eating and how much this was fuelling my stress response. Today if you were to dig through my handbag, you'll find at least two snacks high in protein and carbohydrates to have anytime I feel a dip in my blood sugar levels. Because of this, I am left with less feelings of anxiety (light-headedness, racing heart, inability to focus) and feel far safer in my body. I'm giving her what she needs, and so I am trusting her – and me – more. This is coming from the girl who said 'I'm not a snacker' only a few months ago. In saying yes to me, I've had to say yes to new versions of me – identities I never thought I'd embrace – all in the name of saying yes to the life I want to live. I want to be vital, and healthy, and thriving. I want to feel stable and grounded and full of life-force energy. I'm starting to observe just how powerful the incremental life shifts can be when we fully commit to them step-by-step over a lifetime, rather than forcing ourselves to make rapid, quick changes to a deadline. I'm here for the slow burn.

CHAPTER 5

Slowing (the F) Down

If you were to plug 'nervous system regulation' into Google, chances are you'll be delivered list upon list of 'must dos' and tried-and-tested techniques for activating the parasympathetic nervous system (I know this, because I did it).

While not a comprehensive list of all practices you can lean on by any stretch, my intention in writing this chapter – capturing proven, trauma-informed practices – is to provide an evidenced and easy-to-access starting point for anyone looking to deepen their relationship with nervous system regulation.

This is a list that you can access at any time, and pull from in the moments of deep upheaval, chronic stress or inflammation or an identity crumble or ego death. Most of these practices do not require money and are safe enough that you will not re-traumatise yourself by sitting the practice.

As somatic therapist Eleanor Danks explains:

> Daily stress relief practices are one type of nervous system support that can help us to complete the cycle of stress by expressing and moving it through the body. If used appropriately, they can be a really powerful tool to express unresolved stress and emotions, as well

as getting rid of any excess adrenaline and cortisol running through our system. They can also be helpful in expanding our 'window of tolerance' because they can build internal evidence for us that we are capable of feeling stress and then coming back to a state of calm. This can help us to build nervous system flexibility and capacity, and can teach us that it is safe to experience high levels of sensation and activation without experiencing overwhelm or collapse.

The important thing when it comes to these practices, however, is not to overdo them. If you have experienced trauma and your window of tolerance is currently very small, then bigger is definitely not better … The key is to start gently, to work with your individual window of tolerance, and to build capacity over time. If in doubt, find a professional who can help guide you.

As someone who has danced in wellness circles for close to a decade, I have tried and tested my fair share of trends. You name it, I've likely done it at least once: from various eating styles to juice fasting; Vedic meditation to guided Insight Timer meditations to a ten-day silent meditation retreat; cacao circles to mushroom journeys to spiking my drinks with blue lotus and frankincense. I live for the weird, the wonderful and the magical. I am as open-minded as they come.

But I am also pragmatic, and I don't go into anything without consideration. I live by trial and error. And rather than nodding in agreement with the latest biohacking wellness guru, I always, *always* lean on a healthy dose of logic, teamed with what feels intuitively right in my body, to make choices around what health, wellness and spiritual practices I introduce into my life.

Especially in a season of healing.

So I decided to take advantage of the multitude of qualified, trauma-informed health practitioners I am grateful enough to have access to in my community. I needed to try these practices on for size, and learn why exactly they were important for someone in my position: someone regaining a sense of identity, someone navigating a desire to truly regulate their baseline nervous system and, perhaps most importantly, someone who needed guidance from practitioners who understood trauma and its healing.

Before you begin, it's important to note that there will be times – maybe you're even feeling it now – where you will tell yourself that doing this work is not as important as all of the other things you have on your to-do lists – especially the things you have to do for other people. I hear you. You may feel overwhelmed by the thought of putting the 'wheels in motion' to really saying yes to you. It's nice in concept, but in actuality? It takes hard work. Remember – we are conditioned to resist what is hard. It feels safer to sit in the familiar.

But how is that going for you, really? Because chances are you wouldn't be reading this book if things were 100 per cent perfect. This work IS hard. It isn't something that comes naturally to anyone with people-pleasing tendencies (don't I know it). But my hope is you have this list to reference BEFORE things get even harder. Before your physical body cries out for rest through disease or illness. Before your mental health spirals because you've not carved out a sliver of your own life for you and you alone. Please learn from my mistakes rather than repeating them for yourself. I promise, with that in mind, these practices are easier to implement than you can imagine.

Here's what I tried, and how you can work with these practices on your own path to healing.

Parasympathetic breathwork

It's of no surprise that breathwork is having a 'moment'.

Breathing is part of the autonomic nervous system, which connects involuntary bodily functions to the rest of the body.[15] Multiple studies have shown the significant impact breathwork can have on regulating the parasympathetic nervous system, minimising stress and anxiety, promoting deeper and better-quality sleep, lowering blood pressure, managing PTSD and even improving digestion and managing pain.[16]

Even so, I have never had a breathwork practice, or even felt an appeal towards one. Even knowing the benefits, it all felt too overwhelming for me. But I figured out that this was due to what I have seen online, which only shows it used in the most extreme ways (such is the nature of Instagram cloutability). I don't want to sit in an ice bath while rapidly breathing through the pain. I know that won't benefit me. And I don't want to sit in a room of strangers, crying and contorting through my trauma. While these modes of regulation may be helpful to some (and I know of many who experience positives in these circumstances), they are not helpful to all. This is why saying yes to you, knowing who you are and what serves you as the unique individual you are, is so important – because it can be the fine line between liberation and re-traumatisation.

I spoke to my friend Benjamin Berry, breathworker and cold exposure facilitator, about why we should be practising

15 www.forbes.com/health/wellness/breathwork
16 www.othership.us/resources/breathwork-benefits

breathwork, and what style of breathing would most benefit someone like me. And, likely, someone like you too.

Here is what he shared:

> As our respiration is an autonomic system and also one we can take full control of, it stands to reason that we then have the ability to alter how we react to these changes within our environments by taking control of our breath, if we are able. Something as simple as breathing with an inhale, hold, exhale, hold, each to a count of four seconds (or box breathing, as it's commonly known) can effectively reverse the onset of a panic attack.
>
> A sustained breathwork practice has the added benefit of applying consistent self-regulation, and toning the muscle memory of the nervous system. When we consistently return to this centre, we train our nervous system to attune itself to this grounded feeling within – it enjoys being here. When we are exposed to stressors, whether internal or external, we can more easily return to a regulated state through our breathwork practice as it's something that has been trained.

When I asked Benjamin about the various breathing styles for those of us coming to the practice from a place of stress or trauma, he explained that simple is best. Energetic breathwork is not a starting point, and is in fact a stressor on the body. When performed untrained, unsupervised or incorrectly, it can potentially have damaging results. So while it is not advised to start your breath practice in a holotropic breathing circle, there are simple, safe practices that are available to us immediately.

He shared:

> These types of breathing practices encourage us to breathe less than the average person. In our society, we are accustomed to breathing too much. Long have we thought that because the body feeds off oxygen, more would be better. It's actually the opposite – if we breathe less oxygen and learn to have a healthier relationship with carbon dioxide, we are now proving that we become healthier and higher functioning humans too (both physically and mentally).
>
> To try it at home, a simple progressive tool I use is triangle breathing into staged box breathing. Anyone can do this and it's best to use nasal breathing only – mouth closed.

Triangle breathing

Do each for four seconds.
Inhale.
Hold.
Exhale.
When this feels comfortable, progress to …

Box breathing

Do each for four seconds.
Inhale.
Hold.
Exhale.
Hold.

When this feels comfortable, progress to box breathing for five seconds each rep, then six seconds and so on.

Benjamin says that eventually you will find you are breathing only a few times per minute, limiting your oxygen intake and becoming more familiar with the feeling of carbon dioxide. This has many and varied benefits for our parasympathetic nervous system, such as such as lowering our heart rate and blood pressure, reducing anxiety and building our mind–body connection.

Note that during these exercises, your oxygen saturation in your blood will barely change. You are completely safe.

Journalling

When I asked Dr Scherina to share a simple practice for anyone wanting to start taking care of their nervous systems, journalling was the top of her list.

'Journalling is such a helpful tool. You learn so much about yourself, you get to witness your own progress and this helps to bring up so many awarenesses that we just haven't been attentive to – our triggers, behaviours, communication style and patterns. We can't heal what we are unaware of,' she said.

If you know me, you know I am a journalling fanatic. I still have my very first journal I kept when I was five. ('Today I am going to play Barbies with Leah.' Cute.) I have kept journals for every life season – puberty and high school, through pregnancy, my infamous Saturn Return (when I ran off to the Edinburgh Fringe Festival in search of the meaning of life) and postpartum.

And then, somewhere along the way, journalling lost its sparkle. Not only did it feel like a chore, but it became stressful. I was journalling less and less, to the point where I couldn't tell you the last time I had a consistent, regular daily (or even weekly) practice. Even my Whoop data currently tracks journalling as a 'hurt'. Why?

I spoke to my friend Daisy Moore – founder of journl. – about this. Her answer is fascinating:

> When we are unpacking trauma, it's important to always ask: where are we on the journey? For one person, writing about their trauma might be very therapeutic but for someone else – like in your case currently – that might be way too much. In psychotherapy, we are consistently assessing where the client is, getting to know them to understand what is enough that they can stay in and tolerate 'the work' and what is too much that their defences will spring up and we've lost them. It's always about discerning and coming back to that curious lens.

So basically, when you are journalling from a place of rumination, or replaying stressful or anxiety-inducing events, this practice can absolutely do more harm than good, because we are fixated on the stress. But it isn't journalling that is the issue; it is the style of journalling that needs adjusting.

It's valid to note here that I am a writer. So while, no, I have not been consistent with my journalling practice, yes, I still write a lot. I'm writing a book, I write on my social media. It's important to recognise that to write is not to journal. Just as there are different kinds of writing (poetry, fiction, non-fiction, copy for sales pages, your shopping list), there are also multiple styles of journalling. So which ones matter?

Daisy explains:

> Gratitude journalling or mind dumping are a great way to start. Simply getting in the practice of writing, experiencing how that feels in your mind and body and beginning to make the practice unique to you. We are using journalling as an active tool to come into the present moment and have a single point of focus.
>
> Mind dumping specifically can be really supportive for someone in a stressed state or struggling to get to sleep, for example. One of our brain's many wonderful tasks is to remember, so when we write things down, it's a permission slip to the mind to let it go, like saying, 'I have written that down so I won't forget.'

I asked Daisy to share with us a simple mind dumping practice that would have a noticeable impact on our nervous systems, especially for those of us who have been feeling resistant to writing.

'You could set a timer for six minutes and simply write without a goal in mind. We are not forcing it; we are simply writing to write and being deeply curious to what comes up and how that might change day to day, moment to moment. I think this free-flowing style of journalling is really supportive, especially if we can remain curious.'

She also shared some simple, effective journalling prompts to use when navigating chronic stress or a big identity collapse.

- When did I notice this change?
- If these feelings were leading me somewhere, where would it be?
- When do you feel most yourself? Consider who you are with, what you are doing, where you might be.
- Living in alignment with my true self would mean that I …

When we write to these prompts, it's key that we start to become curious about our current situation, and open to the words that flow through. If you notice that fear arises in sitting this practice, try not to take on too much. Just sit with one of the prompts, rather than the entire list. Play some music that you love. Light a candle. Buy yourself a beautiful new notebook and pen you love to write with (the little things are actually the big things!). Set the space so that you feel comfortable and safe. And know that even if a word or two is all that lands on the page, what matters most is your intention to show up to this practice. It does get easier the more you carve out the space to sit. Give yourself the time you need for the words to flow.

Music

Fun fact about me – when I'm driving, you will always catch me singing at the top of my lungs. I don't listen to podcasts or tune in to audiobooks. I choose music every time. When I'm cleaning the house – it's music. When I'm getting ready for the day ahead – it's music. When I'm setting up my room to write – music. Music. Music. Music.

Perhaps it's because I come from a musical family. Most of my extended family are professional musicians. My brother is a professional singer and musical director. My first ever work-experience job was assistant to Marcia Hines on *Australian Idol* (who is a family friend – let me name-drop, she'll love it). Music is one of my deepest and greatest loves, and I choose it before most other points of joy. So you bet I got excited when I learned – ironically, through Andrew Huberman's podcast, Huberman Lab – that music is a proven point of nervous system regulation.

In fact, it is said that listening to your favourite music for 10 to 60 minutes a day can see profound impacts on your nervous system response, including a reduced RHR, an increase in HRV and even activating features of your parasympathetic nervous system.[17]

A study conducted by *Science Direct* showed that, overall, there is a positive impact on HRV when it comes to listening to music,[18] with this particular study showing enhanced parasympathetic activity. The rule of thumb being: listen to music that makes you feel good.

Now, I am someone who absolutely lives for music that stirs emotion. It's the poet in me. Trent constantly complains how depressing my music choices are, but for me, I want something that makes me feel. However, reviewing this research, I realised that perhaps my repeated acoustic sad folk music wasn't doing me any solids in this current life season. While I love this style more than anything (shout out to Noah Kahan), maybe it was time to lean on my old faithful playlist – aptly titled my *High Vibes* playlist (think 90s/early noughties pop hits).

So I swapped out my playlist choices, and I have to say, I forgot how good it feels to start my day singing and dancing in the kitchen. There's a noticeable lightness in my energy that I carry with me in the day ahead. In fact, this was a component I taught

17 podcastnotes.org/huberman-lab/how-to-use-music-to-boost-motivation-mood-improve-learning-huberman-lab
18 www.sciencedirect.com/science/article/pii/S1050173821000700

my clients years ago specifically for manifestation practices. That to cultivate positive energy, it was as simple as moving and singing to our favourite music. This experience has been like connecting with an old friend again, and it's a practice that I know changes my life whenever I lean on it.

The other style of music I lean on when I am stressed, and perhaps not feeling called to upbeat tracks, is 528hz music. Often referred to as the 'love frequency' or the 'vibration of love', 528hz frequency is deeply associated with healing. Chlorophyll (in plants) vibrates at this frequency. Bees buzz at this magical frequency to pollinate flowers. And the air we breathe is made up of this exact number of hertz.[19]

Sceptic or not, the healing qualities of 528hz music have been proven by science, with a reduction in anxiety displayed in rats after prolonged exposure.[20]

I like to use 528hz music when I am winding down for the day – I pair it with my box breathing and play it through Spotify (just search '528 hertz') for ten minutes. That's all it takes. I also love resting in a warm bath or showering to this music. Save your high vibes playlist for driving and your frequency music for winding down at the end of the day.

Meditation

Now, this has been an interesting one. Not dissimilar to my journalling experience, when I stepped into motherhood, my relationship with meditation fell by the wayside. Likely at a time I needed it most, I dropped the ball – and it's been a challenging one to pick back up.

19 www.news10.com/business/press-releases/ein-presswire/589107523/the-benefits-of-aligning-with-the-528-hz-frequency
20 pubmed.ncbi.nlm.nih.gov/30414050

My normal practice of choice – a Vedic one – started to feel far more stressful than easeful. In the space I had free, I didn't want to sit and launder my stress. I wanted to rest and feel liberated from stress. In my mind, there was a difference. I wanted to cut out the noise and get straight to peace. And in doing so, I have been actively avoiding sitting in any space of 'discomfort' – which ironically has resulted in more prolonged discomfort as time has gone on and I've walked further and further away from my practice.

So, what's the deal? Are there certain kinds of meditation that are more beneficial to our nervous system than others?

Meditation, especially a practice like transcendental meditation (which my Vedic practice falls into), is proven to activate the parasympathetic nervous system and quieten the sympathetic nervous system.[21] Plain and simple, meditation is a nervous system regulator.

In fact, any practice that allows you to stop and focus on the breath is going to have a positive impact on your nervous system. But if you're wanting to really nurture your parasympathetic nervous system, then a regular transcendental practice seems to be the way to go. That is, 20 minutes, twice a day, ongoing. Morning and afternoon. Repetition and consistency are vital.

Not only does a regular meditation practice support your autonomic nervous system, it also improves relaxation, regulates your emotional state and allows for increased awareness.[22] There really is a reason why everyone bangs on about it.

For me, I find my practice is one of the first things to drop – even though I know it's good for me – because when life is

21 sitn.hms.harvard.edu/flash/2009/issue61
22 mindworks.org/blog/meditation-autonomic-nervous-system

full, my meditation practice also feels full. I'm laundering more stress, so these sittings are less peaceful and more active. My mind races. Twenty minutes feel like hours. I'd rather scroll Insta.

This is where consistency is so important. The nature of a transcendental meditation practice lies in the busier, more 'active' sits, because this is where we are actively regulating our systems. Practising meditation isn't supposed to feel quiet and still every time. The gift lies in sitting through the discomfort of the active mind, not in turning it off (because can we ever?). The thoughts we have during our practice is stress being siphoned from the nervous system. Without the thoughts, there is no regulation!

We are lucky to have a smorgasbord of guided meditation apps and platforms available at the click of a button – a simple search for 'parasympathetic meditation' will have you inundated with options. If you already have your own meditation practice, absolutely stick to it. And when you feel the call or have the space to, you can add on a transcendental practice as you go. This is not a one-or-the-other approach. Meditation in all ways is beneficial. However, when it comes to deep nervous system regulation, you will see the deepest and most profound results with a regular Transcendental or Vedic practice, which can only be taught from a Transcendental or Vedic meditation teacher.

Decluttering

While not necessarily a nervous system regulatory practice per se, living in a cluttered space has been proven to increase cortisol levels, having a direct impact on our stress response. And if we relate an increase in cortisol levels to an increasingly stressed nervous system,[23] then perhaps this is a 'low hanging fruit' we can pick when our systems are in dire need of support.

Part of my accumulated stress in new motherhood were the piles of dishes in the sink begging to be washed, adding to my daily stress toll every day. It's only in the past month – after living here more than three years – that we've had a dishwasher installed and I can tell you point-blank, no exaggeration, that this has changed my life.

For some of us, establishing a deeper relationship with cleanliness will look like getting help by way of a cleaner, should our financial position allow this for us. For others, this will depend on our definition of 'clutter'. Whether you've jumped on the Marie Kondo train or not, there is much wisdom in her teachings. In her book *The Life-Changing Magic of Tidying Up*, Kondo shares how creating a space that 'sparks joy' will positively impact your life in a multitude of ways.

Fun fact about me: if you were to ask me one of my not-so-strong points, it would absolutely be that I am not a clean freak. I'm not messy (she says defensively) but ask Trent and he will absolutely vouch that I don't put things in their proper place, and storage solutions are not my strong point (I prefer to shove things in a drawer and forget about them).

With that said, I'm willing to put myself and my idiosyncrasies on the line in the name of research and so – naturally – I signed up to Marie Kondo's Fundamentals of Tidying course. This course significantly changed the game for me. I learned everything from folding styles to what 'sparking joy'

23 www.ncbi.nlm.nih.gov/books/NBK541120

actually means, to where to even start when it comes to totally decluttering your home and creating more beauty in your life.

How do I feel? Well, I'll put it plain and simple – I fold my undies now. Yep. This former drawer-stuffer is no longer a clutter queen. The feeling of satisfaction I get when I open my cupboard now is something I did not anticipate. And I know this is having a profound effect on my nervous system too. My spaces are clean, my clothes are all pieces I genuinely feel good in and this seemingly 'little' piece of my day creates a massive ripple effect across all elements of my life. I started in my bedroom, and have now decluttered my kitchen and my car, with the office next on my hit list. I'm a woman on a mission and that mission is to clean. I'm practically Monica in *Friends*. It's been a real game-changer for me.

That said, I don't think I had the window of tolerance to start this process when I did. There is a LOT of mess to sit in before the cleanliness – and because of this, I navigated a messy room with piles upon piles of clothes I was sorting for close to a month. I genuinely didn't have the energy to sit in the mess. That was a very stressful experience for me (and my neat-freak husband) and, in hindsight, I would have waited for my stress levels to have been a little more stable before diving into the process.

This is a practice to look at when you feel you have the space, time and energy for the work, because physical labour is a part of it. If you currently do not have the energetic capacity to overhaul your home environment, focus on the other practices in this chapter instead and wait until you start to feel you have more in your bandwidth to dive in.

Beauty

Yes – you read that correctly! When I sat to write this part of the book, I knew I was going to include the concept of beauty. That is, anything aesthetically pleasing, that is moving to the sensory body (smell, sight, sound, touch and/or taste). I have found so much peace in cultivating a life with my version of beauty at the forefront – fresh cut flowers from our garden, baking from scratch, spritzing a scented mist, lighting incense and candles, a home filled with eclectic art, surrounded by trees. It felt important – vital even – that I spoke to beauty as a healer. What I didn't realise is that this concept is an entire branch of neuroscience; beauty really, truly regulates our nervous systems.

Neuroaesthetics is a relatively recently coined subcategory of neuroscience that specifically looks at the biological mechanisms involved in our experiences with beauty.[24]

While there is still limitation in the research pertaining to neuroaesthetics (namely, beauty being a subjective experience that is near impossible to be defined across the board), there is growing evidence to suggest that our experience of beauty absolutely correlates to positive shifts in our brains.

Semir Zeki, Professor of Neuroaesthetics at University College London says that activity in the medial prefrontal cortex is stronger when you think something is beautiful.[25] It is also evidenced that emotions play a large role in the experience of aesthetics due to the personal and subjective nature of perception.[26]

So, rather than getting caught up in the philosophical versus scientific debate around what beauty is (although, it would

24 www.sciencedirect.com/topics/psychology/neuroaesthetics
25 www.thecrimson.com/article/2017/11/10/neuroaesthetics-cover
26 www.artsmentalhealth.org/neuroaesthetics

make for a fun dinner party conversation), let's agree that feeling a sense of beauty absolutely has a positive impact on our brains. It can even lower our cortisol levels. As an example, Dr Nancy Etcoff, Assistant Clinical Professor in Psychology at Harvard Medical School, conducted a behavioural research study proving that people with fresh cut flowers in their home feel more compassionate toward others and feel less depressed, anxious and worried.[27]

So if we were to define beauty as 'the combination of all the qualities of a person or thing that delight the senses and please the mind',[28] then there is very real evidence to suggest that beauty is a nervous system regulator. The research may not have totally caught up yet, but it is really only a matter of time.

Further to this, if we were to look at beauty in the context of our environment, design that doesn't make sense to your brain or is displeasing, clutter and spaces which make you feel disconnected can all trigger the sympathetic nervous system and lead to mental distress.[29]

Coherent design and beauty trigger the parasympathetic response, leading to a more balanced homeostasis within the nervous system and a greater degree of mental health.[30]

The biggest question here for us now is: how do we personally define beauty?

When I think of beauty, I am instantly taken to the five senses and how they respond to certain stimuli. While most neuroaesthetic research predominantly focuses on visual art (what we see, and therefore how we feel/react based on the visual stimuli), for the sake of multifaceted beauty, let's consider all stimuli.

27 safnow.org/aboutflowers/quick-links/health-benefits-research/home-ecology-of-flowers-study
28 www.collinsdictionary.com/dictionary/english/beauty
29 www.pippinhomedesigns.com/you-inspired-living/science_of_a_happy_home
30 www.pippinhomedesigns.com/you-inspired-living/science_of_a_happy_home

Connecting with beauty

Take a moment to connect in with the following prompts, across all of your senses …

Beautiful sights?
Beautiful smells?
Beautiful sounds?
Beautiful textures?
Beautiful tastes?

Now that you have clearly identified your own version of beauty, consider how you can bring more of these pieces into your home and work environments. How can you cultivate more of a beautiful life?

Emotional freedom technique (EFT)

If you read my first book, you may remember that I mentioned the benefits of EFT when tending to your energetic wellbeing. What I didn't touch on were the proven statistics when it comes to regular EFT (otherwise known as 'tapping') and its direct correlation to nervous system regulation, because I didn't even realise it at the time. Regular tapping is one of the most gentle and profound methods you can lean on for activating the parasympathetic nervous system.

Proven clinical EFT markers for nervous system regulation include a 37 per cent drop in cortisol levels, a 40 per cent drop in anxiety, 35 per cent drop in depression, 32 per cent drop in PTSD symptoms, 57 per cent drop in pain and a 113 per cent increase in immune system markers and 31 per cent increase in happiness.[31]

31 www.petastapleton.com/free-eft-resources

I've enjoyed dropping into a tapping sesh over the years, only really leaning on it as a last resort when times are really challenging. I didn't consider it a necessary means for ongoing practice – I thought it was only a tool I needed when I was 'too far gone'. However, noting these drastic shifts in nervous system markers, I sat with my friend and accredited EFT practitioner Erin Laishley to come up with a plan of attack to support my nervous system.

We decided to meet once a fortnight to process whatever stress I was feeling. Some sessions, I would come to Erin with a clear idea of exactly what I wanted to 'tap' on – themes like having a big health flare or feeling run-down and exhausted. However, just as often were moments I had absolutely no idea what we would work on that session. These were actually the sessions that felt the most powerful, because it gave me an opportunity to get out of my mind and into the sensations my body wanted to feel and process.

Erin talked me through how EFT actually works, and why it is that emotion is likely to emerge in a session. She shared:

> What many people don't realise is that EFT is a remarkable technique that can be used to heal and release trauma from your physical, emotional and energetic body.
>
> When we tap, we send a soothing signal to the amygdala in the brain, which creates a feeling of safety and calm in our body. This feeling of safety is key and is especially effective when you're working with past trauma, PTSD or similar, as you're rewiring your brain's stress pattern and disarming the cortisol response.

Let's say you have a memory from childhood of being teased and whenever you think back on this memory, you feel an emotional charge such as anxiety, sweaty palms or a feeling of heaviness in your body. This memory triggers a stress response, which is wired to protect you, even when there is no danger present. So, how do we change that stress signal? We tap!

Emotional memories are like onions – they're layered, so it's important you stay focused on what's coming up for you to fully clear the stories and beliefs you may be harbouring. My advice is to always keep track of the emotion you're feeling, and any physical sensations in the body. So, when you tune into the memory, you might start feeling anxious in your heart space – tap and clear that. Then you might feel some anger – tap and clear that. Sadness – tap and clear that. Shame. Fear. Regret. Tap and clear each layer.

And so on and so forth. Rinse and repeat, following the threads of emotion until finally you reach a place of peace. Maybe you feel neutral, a sense of acceptance or perhaps you sense a shift in your perspective. But you will notice, when reflecting back, things look and feel *different*.

What I found after my own regular commitment to tapping was that my stress levels would drop to their lowest measured state during a session, followed by an increase (positive surge) in my recovery the day after a session. Not to mention that for all of the emotional releasing, I was left feeling lighter and with more clarity.

'This is the power of EFT,' Erin shared with me. 'Safely, gently and effectively it allows us to disarm the hold that these past events and memories can have on us. From small traumas, to big ones, it is possible to retrain our brain and nervous system so that we don't feel "triggered", and so that the old beliefs and stories we've inherited about ourselves can change and shift. It truly is remarkable, powerful work.'

If you're curious about starting your own EFT practice, there are a multitude of free practices available on apps like Insight Timer and even YouTube. Seeking out a practitioner you trust – like me with Erin – can also be a wonderful place to start, either in a one-on-one capacity, or via their own online tapping resources. I love Erin's work so much that she contributes EFT practices to my online membership ongoing.

Chiropractic care

The final piece of the puzzle, not to be diluted or dismissed, is that of chiropractic care. Where nervous system speak is relatively new in the scheme of pop-culture rhetoric, these conversations have been standard practice in chiropractic circles for decades.

In fact, when I asked Dr Scherina to share the most overlooked/underrated practices for true nervous system regulation, chiropractic care was the top of her list.

> As much as I talk about nervous system regulation, I still believe chiropractic is so overlooked when it comes to truly healing.

> Chiropractors have been around for over 100 years and are trained specifically to work with the nervous system. I believe the reason being is because of the verbiage used to explain chiropractic – usually you hear 'pain' is why you seek a chiropractor and that's just not our foundation. While yes, chiropractic does help tremendously to relieve pain, the work goes so much deeper when it comes to healing and the nervous system. Going to a chiropractor for pain is like going to a dentist just for cleaning when we all know we go to a dentist for much more than that.

I spoke to my chiropractor, Dr Regan Osborne, for his take. He shared:

> The nervous system is the communication highway between Body, Mind and Spirit, with the gut being the physical anchor, or seat of the spirit. We are each of these things individually yet simultaneously, inextricably intertwined. Any stress that we encounter – or hold – affects and is reflected in the function of each of these aspects of self via the nervous system as it learns and remembers these adaptations.
>
> Bodywork, as is the basis of most chiropractors, is one aspect of the healing or regulatory journey. We would argue though, that because of the nervous system's role in communication and the direct impact chiropractic care has on that, that it is indeed a very necessary, if not the most necessary aspect.

When I was pregnant, I visited my chiropractor, Dr Megan Osborne (Regan's wife – can we take a moment for their rhyming names?), every week. That is, from week 13 of pregnancy to week 39, just before I went into labour, and then right afterwards, when my little girl was only one week old (Megan came to our home to work on me). There is a huge public misconception on what chiropractic care actually entails (I rarely – if ever – had my 'back cracked' and was more often treated at a much subtler, gentler level, especially during pregnancy). In my opinion, chiropractic care was one of the major reasons I experienced such a vibrant and healthy pregnancy.

Dr Scherina adds, 'I would say it's important to find a chiropractor that is nervous system-focused since there are some that do enjoy focusing on athletes, pain, car accidents etc.'

While I strongly believe in chiropractic support from a nervous system perspective – and have experienced the evidence of it myself – this is also a practice that involves regular financial investment. It is the practice I have neglected the most (one session in three months) due to financial strains. I think it's important to share this; while there are multiple practices available to us for true and deep nervous system support and healing, we can only ever access what is within our reach – financially, accessibly or otherwise. If anything puts you into financial strain, it is not serving your nervous system. There are many modalities available to us that do not require a financial outlay. Start there and build on those, once you are ready and able. In an ideal world, I would see my chiropractor every fortnight. For now, it is when finances allow, and I concentrate on other practices.

ACTIVITY: **Your hit list**

So now that you have your hit list of effective and easy nervous system practices, how can you weave them into your day?

I love to pair mine together as often as possible. Some examples:

- To wind down at the end of the day, I play my 528hz music, and practise my box breathing.
- Repeat the above, but in the bath (add some rose petals and essential oils to tick beauty off the list too!).
- Clean out your wardrobe while playing your high vibes playlist.
- Eat your nourishing breakfast while the morning sun hits your face.
- Journal immediately following your EFT practice.
- Journal immediately after meditating.

Add yours below:

The options are endless and, as you can see, also require very minimal time and financial investment.

Something to remember:

If you start by focusing on nourishment, sleep, fresh air and a clean home environment – let that be enough.

If you decide you have your baselines sorted, and it's time to pick up a breath or meditation practice – let that be enough.

If you are ready to dive a little deeper and enlist the support of a chiropractor or EFT coach – let that be enough.

Your journey to slowing down is not a set-and-forget approach. Depending on the twists and turns on the path you are walking, you will require a smorgasbord of options to navigate it with confidence. Rather than getting bogged-down by the noise and overwhelmed by the options, come back to the basics.

Nourishment. Sleep. The breath. The sun. Your environment. Your senses. Beauty.

Everything else will follow.

ACTIVITY: **My personal slow-down practices**

Take a moment to reflect on each of the nervous system practices shared in this chapter, and use these questions as journalling prompts:

Which practices stand out to you most? Why do you think that is?

What is the easiest way you can introduce ONE practice into your day-to-day life ongoing?

Are there practices you are already implementing? How could you elevate these practices or take them to the next level? (e.g. change weekly journalling to every three days)

I have to laugh, because as I'm researching this book, I'm finding myself being reminded of what I already know. I was meditating consistently back when I wrote my first book because I knew it was good for me. But like most things, when we drop a ball, even though we know the ball is good for us, picking it up again is the hardest part. People pleasers are conditioned to overcomplicate things, when the reality of slowing down is really quite simple, and often lies in the things we are most avoiding.

I was halfway through writing this book (seven weeks, to be exact) when my health took a real turn. I'd spent the previous month making the big and not-so-big adjustments to my daily life – all of the pieces I've listed here, homing in on my physical body. I'd been working with Chantel for close to a month, implementing all of the supplements, doing my breathwork practices, improving my sleep hygiene, getting my morning sun.

I was meeting with Erin for EFT fortnightly, I'd seen Megan my chiropractor for a long overdue adjustment, I was nourishing my body with regular, balanced meals. I decluttered my bedroom and had fresh flowers in every room of my home. I was more focused on my wellbeing than I've been in years. And the markers were starting to trend in the positive direction – my RHR was decreasing, my HRV was soaring, my sleep quality was deepening.

Then, seemingly out of nowhere, my health took a dive.

Okay, let's be real – it absolutely plummeted.

It all started after a morning of cacao and pickled beetroots. Now, these weren't the only things on my plate, but they were absolutely the culprit of what occurred next: a histamine reaction all over my face and neck. This histamine reaction isn't unheard of for me – the last time I experienced something similar was when I was navigating health challenges postpartum. But it was more intense than I've ever experienced before. In fact, as I write this two weeks later, I still have inflamed, puffy eyes and rashing skin on my face and neck.

But that wasn't the half of it. Oh no. After making the necessary adjustments to my diet (a low-histamine diet is not something I'd wish on anyone, I might add), I was expecting to notice a clear-up within a week, max. Because I was doing all of the right things. I was listening to my body. I was slowing down. (I was writing the book about it, FFS!) I knew the things and had all of the right people in my corner. So why didn't things shift?

Well, they did shift … the wrong way. Things actually got worse. My bleed arrived on day 35, a heavy, clotty mess, with a fun dose of migraine that left me bedridden for three days, unable to open my eyes because of the pain. As well as the rash on my face and the inflammation around my eyes, I developed a localised rash on my thyroid. Almost as if my body was shouting at me, 'Look here, Hollie! This is what you need to focus on!'

And while I was very aware of my body doing her best to shed whatever was wanting to move through me, I also had very little to give anyone, myself included. Getting out of bed was a challenge, let alone still showing up to mother my two-year-old. Forget writing this book – it was so bad, I had to take a week off everything.

At the same time, my phone broke. Out of nowhere. I wasn't even using it, it just started flashing white one random evening while I was watching *Friends* in bed (my comfort show of choice). It seemed even my technology was trying to send me signs.

Then, two weeks into this clusterfuck of health upheaval, I caught a virus. Way to kick a girl when she's down. At my worst in all of this, I was begging and pleading to the powers that be to please, please help me heal. To please take the pain away. To please give me back my health.

I felt weak. Helpless. Hopeless.

And then … something happened.

I was napping with my little girl – the heaviness in my limbs were crying for rest on this day, and I hardly had any voice left – when I woke up with this sense of impending urgency. I couldn't place it at all, other than I no longer needed to nap; I needed to write.

And so I opened my replacement phone from the repair shop and, without even thinking, I started writing in the Notes app:

Who I am becoming …

What followed this prompt was a stream-of-consciousness trail of thought, inspired idea and actions to take as I step into this new iteration of me. And as I wrote, clarity arrived. The new version of me has her voice heard in a whole new way, so *of course* my throat is needing to recalibrate. Of course my thyroid is needing to heal. The new version of me I am wanting to step into has a whole new approach to her career – so *of course* there are parts of me needing to fall away energetically.

Of course.

This new version of me I am stepping into is stepping in front of the camera, to be seen in my physical body in ways I haven't stepped into in years now. So *of course* the literal skin on my face needs to shed, my eyes need to refocus on a new vision, and my whole system needs to rest for what's to come.

Of course.

Here's the thing. We are body, and we are soul. And both of these parts of us require just as much tending to as the other. It is our responsibility to ourselves to catch when we have swung too far one way, or the other. Or maybe completely dismissed one for the other. For me, when I started to write this book, I had completely dismissed the physical, with a hyper-focus on the soul. I was all about healing metaphysically, but physically? No thank you.

Now? My hyperfixation on the physical – on regulating my nervous system, and healing from my trauma – left my body crying, begging and pleading for me to bring my physical focus into harmony with the soul. I need both. We all do.

And that is why it will never be enough to just focus on the physical. The nervous system regulating. The nutrition and the movement.

That is only half of the puzzle.

The other half lies in tuning in.

CHAPTER 6

Somatic Therapy and Your Energetic Toolkit

I woke up this morning in a funk. I know we all have these mornings, and it probably isn't coincidental that I'm at day 27 of my cycle (IYKYK) and we're on the precipice of the Scorpio Full Moon (astro-girl things), but no matter 'what' the cause of these 'big feelings' (as I describe them to my toddler), the reality is: today I woke up feeling big feelings. Think deep guttural rage followed by an overwhelming sadness that I couldn't place, and couldn't shake. I felt myself withdraw from my husband, become snappy with our little girl and mope around at the start of the day with rage-clean mode activated: corners of the home that usually didn't bother me all of a sudden needed to be cleaned up RIGHT NOW or life as I knew it would surely implode.

I needed space. Cleanliness. And everyone to stop looking at me and talking to me for at least five minutes.

I was overstimulated. Overwhelmed. And, quite frankly, over it.

It was when I noticed my little girl experiencing similar 'big feelings' (that she was likely mirroring from me) that I caught myself directing her to the pillow we use to 'move them out' – through punching and sounding, mostly. I know without question how to hold my little girl through these very normal, very natural emotions that prefer to move out of our bodies than stay in. So why wasn't I holding myself?

When our nanny arrived for my three-hour writing block, the easiest thing in the world would have been for me to dive straight into writing to make the most of the time we had, having her help me as I write. I only have limited hours of care – six a week, in fact – when I can write this book. And I don't know if you know this, but six hours a week of writing time, with a three-and-a-half-month book deadline, isn't much. Every hour counts. So me diving straight into it would have made the most sense, not just logically, but from a business perspective. More time equals more words equals more likely to make my deadline.

But this isn't about logic. This is about feeling. Tuning in. And being okay with the things that don't often make sense.

And so, rather than dive into work and push this funk I woke with down deeply, only to be confronted by it at a later (likely unanticipated, and probably highly inconvenient) date, I decided today I would fully feel whatever wanted to come through first, before doing anything else. I would give myself the space and the time to actually tune in.

This is why tuning in is so key to saying yes to ourselves, and not necessarily the palatable and beautiful parts of ourselves (they're easy to say yes to, after all!), but the messy, inexplicable parts we'd prefer to avoid.

Having a go-to practice to move emotion and energy through isn't just for our children to move their big feelings through. It's for us, too.

And for me, my practice almost always starts with connecting with my heart. I do this with cacao. The plant medicine of the heart, ceremonial cacao is known to the ancient Mayan culture as 'the food of the gods'.[32] One of the highest known sources of magnesium and calcium, drinking ceremonial cacao in ritual or sacred ceremony activates feelings of heart coherence. When we are functioning in a state of heart coherence, our breathing slows alongside our heartbeat, and this state promotes deep feelings of gratitude and an overwhelming sense of love. Overall, sitting with cacao in a ceremonial context is highly supportive of our emotional wellbeing.

This morning, I chose to prepare myself a mug of cacao infused with frankincense (known for its grounding qualities) and blue lotus (for heart activation). I prepared my cacao slowly to one of my favourite playlists, used my heart activation mist to bring in scent as an anchor point (more on this soon), and rugged up in my most comfortable hoodie (that also happens to be Taylor Swift merch, reserve your judgements here). I made sure each of my senses were activated to bring me into full presence. I could smell the layers of cacao mixed with lavender and rose from my heart spray, I could feel the warmth of my hoodie on my skin, and the mug underneath my fingertips, I could hear the music in my ears, I could see my dimly lit and clean ceremony space, complete with my altar, fresh flowers and my vision board, and I was about to taste my cacao.

32 www.anchoringthelight.com/sacred-chocolate

Each anchor point is strategically placed to bring me into full present-moment awareness, which is essential if you're truly willing to meet yourself in the process of feeling your feelings.

Now, I am lucky enough that I run my own ceremonial membership, The Heart Space, and have a backlog of hours upon hours of ceremonies and rituals to choose to sit at my own leisure. Ceremonies for heart opening, ceremonies for grieving, ceremonies for cultivating joy. I founded The Heart Space (in the very early stages of new motherhood, no less) because I realised how vital it is to sit in regular ritual connecting with our hearts, and to move emotion through our bodies – how incredibly transformative it can be to our whole lives – and how few of us have a regular practice like this to turn to.

In adulthood, when the big feelings come, where do they go? More often than not, they don't go anywhere. We don't want to feel them. Discomfort is highly inconvenient, and big emotion is 'cringe' after all. (Not really, but society tells us it is, so it must be true, right?)

And so we continue to 'get on with it'. Mask the pain, smile through the wrong-side-of-the-bed days and wonder why, as a collective, we are becoming sicker, not to mention more disconnected from our hearts and our intuition.

I truly believe the answer lies in regular ritual – specifically, in sitting with our hearts.

This morning's practice was the circuit-breaker I needed to move 'stuck' energy through. I sat, I sipped, I journalled, I moved my body and then – once the energy felt safe enough to move – I cried. Bawled, in fact. Deep guttural wails.

Underneath my wrong-side-of-the-bed morning was something so much deeper. I have been suppressing grief – the reality of us needing to make a very upsetting decision in putting our dog, Archie, to sleep. But I hadn't wanted to look at that, so I'd suppressed it. Avoided it. And in avoiding it, I'd pushed down the feeling, deeper and deeper. And we know by now that the more we do this, the more inclined it is to pile up on top of other suppressed emotions until, one day, we experience a tidal wave of everything we were once too afraid to feel.

I'm done with the tidal waves. I'm willing to feel it all now – no matter how deeply, no matter how raw, no matter how awful – because I know this is living fully. Living fully lies in living in the polarity; in the light and the shade. You cannot just shine brightly for shining's sake. To fully shine means you are also willing to meet your darkness when it arises. The brighter a light you cast, the darker the shadow that falls, after all. And it doesn't make it easy, not by a long shot. But it does mean that in your courage to face the flames of alchemy head-on, the intensity subsides far quicker than if you were to suppress it all in a carefully orchestrated avoidance pattern.

As the saying goes: better out than in. This is truth when it comes to our emotional bodies. We MUST have emotional regulatory practices that move emotions out of the body.
To truly thrive, these means are not just nice-to-haves, and absolutely not just 'woo-woo' practices with no substance (I hate that term by the way, but we can talk about why it dilutes the power of energetics and our relationship to our innate intuitive wisdom another time).

It lies in somatic healing. That is – applying mind-body healing to aid in trauma recovery. And the beauty is – science is catching up.

Naturally, I took my (somewhat limited) understanding of somatic therapy (meaning: 'of the body') to Eleanor Danks, to gauge an understanding of this approach to healing the mind and the body, by moving emotion out and through.

She explains:

> While traditional talk therapies focus purely on the mind (primarily our thoughts, beliefs, and stories), somatic therapy views the mind and body as a connected whole, and places an equal importance on both. Somatic therapies work primarily with our experience of sensation, emotion, and energy in the body, and uses techniques such as the breath, movement, and physical touch to process past and present experiences and re-pattern the coping mechanisms that the body has learned.
>
> Once we understand that trauma is the internal experience we have in reaction to an external event/s, we can understand that trauma is an inherently physiological experience made up of sensations, emotions and energy. Many of these internal experiences are non-verbal, meaning they don't have language attached to them, and can therefore be very difficult to process through talk therapy only. Working with the body through somatic therapy means that we can work directly with these internal experiences, therefore

> targeting the source of the trauma directly, rather than trying to think or talk ourselves through it.
>
> When we work directly with the body, we are able to give the body the experience of completing cycles of stress and emotion that have been interrupted or frozen previously, which helps us to digest these past experiences. It also enables us to give the body real-time experiences of felt safety, which is far more effective than trying to convince our mind that we are safe through words alone.

While I've already shared somatic practices like breathwork and EFT, which are powerful tools to move stagnant and unexpressed emotion and energy through the body (often under the guidance of a trauma-informed practitioner), there are a multitude of somatic, energetic-focused practices available to support your journey, no matter if it's deep trauma you are desiring to move through, or simply some 'sticky' energy that is not yours.

These tools are vital for everyone, no matter your daily life, as we all feel deeply. If we are not allowing ourselves the full space to honour these feelings, we run the risk of them erupting outside of our control at a later date, be it through an emotional outburst, or physical ailment, like me currently (or both).

The funny thing is that this way of healing has always been my favoured method. Put it down to years of being gaslit by medical practitioners (I know I'm not the only one), or perhaps that my own line of work is deeply entrenched in all things energy, spirituality and the 'unseen realms', but without even knowing what I was doing, I have always sought somatic practices for my healing. As I've said many times before, Louise Hay's *You Can Heal Your Life* is my bible.

I know how to muscle-test to clear my energy field. I've been receiving reiki and kinesiology as a self-care practice for more than a decade. My bodywork practitioner is practically on speed dial. I have a cupboard of homeopathic tinctures and flower remedies for everything from unlocking sexual lifeforce energy, to dealing with 'bum worms' (I have a two-year-old, remember?). I've tremor-released in therapy sessions for hours at a time. During my marathon labour, my doula was practising kinesiology on me mid-contractions.

I am not afraid of somatics. I know the power of this way of healing. It works. And I am so grateful to have a multitude of practitioners at my disposal to hold me through these shifts. But as I said at the end of the previous chapter, I've been hit with the realisation that healing doesn't lie in just one basket. We are body AND soul. Physical vessel AND energy. And if you're focusing only on the body, or only on the spirit – one will have some catching up to do. You simply cannot have one without the other.

This was my experience when first sitting opposite Chantel, bemoaning that my test results had not miraculously pointed to my healing, but were indicating a regression. I genuinely didn't expect this, because I had leaned on the somatics. I had done so much work! I had sat the family constellation sessions (more on that in the tremor-releasing section below), I'd had hours upon hours of bodywork releasing my childhood traumas, I'd sat in shadow work therapy where my body shook involuntarily on the couch for hours. I joined all of the energetic dots. I cleared my field daily. I ended relationships I never wanted to. I upheld strong boundaries. I said 'no' more than I ever had before.

I spoke my deepest, most vulnerable fears aloud and took tinctures to hold me through grief and shame. I chose joy in my life. I felt creatively fulfilled again.

But I neglected to look at my physical body. I didn't take my blood tests to a practitioner who could have provided me with supplements to support my healing. I stopped seeing my chiro. I picked and chose, and picked and chose and picked and chose, because we only have limited time and limited money (especially in this day and age, am I right?) and so my preference was on the deep, soul-healing stuff. That's what called me. Tuning in. And that isn't wrong.

But as I sat opposite Chantel, and she asked me what protocol I had started following my last round of bloods that showed my markers were starting to decline, the penny dropped. I was doing the healing in reverse.

She confirmed this for me, that most clients who come to her are far more willing to go on another gut cleanse, another thyroid supplement, another meal plan, another ice bath. Give them anything other than actually needing to look at the depths of their soul: the heavy lifting required here is often too much to bear.

Me? I did it in reverse. I don't run from the depths – I dive straight in (unless it's an ice bath, in which case, I'll pass). I was doing all of the heavy lifting with no baseline foundation in my physical body. My body was crying out for me to slow down on the energy front and wait for it to catch up.

And this is where I'm at now. Taking my very human supplements (currently nine different types a day), lying on the couch with my very human castor oil heat pack, eating my very human meals at my very human scheduled hours every day, having my very human naps, wearing my very human biometric tracker to track my very human health markers.

That said, I am also aware that I have currently swung too far the other way. I have been so focused on regulating my nervous system, tracking my data and expanding my HRV that I've completely neglected the part of me that still needs the energetic healing in equal measure. I thrive joining the alchemical dots and understanding the metaphysical underneath the physical. And I'm currently learning that it is not a one-or-the-other approach – it must be both.

We need to slow down and listen to our physical bodies, get our foundations straight and work on our nervous systems just as much as we need to tune in and start responding to the signs our energetic bodies are sending us. We are body AND spirit. Mind AND soul. And it's vital that we tend to both in equal measure.

So, how do we do it? Where do we begin? It's far more commonplace to know where to go when we need our bloods tested, or our supplements prescribed. But what about our energetic vitals? Where do we go to tend to this part of our body?

Is it as simple as implementing a daily cacao ritual? I mean, that's a lovely way to start, but the truth is there are many powerful energetic modalities that are vital for our full-spectrum healing.

–

It would be remiss of me to not make note of the very commonly referenced nervous system regulatory practices that I have intentionally excluded from these chapters. Things like extreme temperature therapies (ice baths and saunas), any form of high-intensity movement, extreme somatic group journeys (encouraging trauma revisitation) and even plant medicine journeys like ayahuasca or psilocybin (which also lend themselves to trauma revisitation when not held appropriately).

This is because these practices do not regulate the majority of people's nervous systems – and can in fact re-traumatise and become far more stress-inducing than intended. Often, the facilitators of these practices are not trauma-informed. This is dangerous and can create more damage for the participant to unravel from.

Dr Scherina echoed my sentiments. When I asked her if there were any practices touted online as nervous system regulators that can actually do more harm than good, she said, 'There are many! Mostly tools of self-regulation like cold plunges, fasting, intense breathwork etc. All of those can be very helpful, but only after the nervous system has been restored to be able to adapt to daily stressors.'

Remember, one person's medicine can often be another's poison. The practices I have shared here are safe for ALL to work with, no matter your health history, level of experience or background. They are trauma-safe, gentle and evidenced in their successes of activating parasympathetic activity and, in turn, truly regulating your nervous system from the ground up.

They are shared with the intention that slowing down and tuning in becomes something easily accessed and safely integrated.

Somatic bodywork

I was sitting with my bodywork practitioner, Asha, prepping for a luxurious two-hour session on her massage table. While not massage alone, a good holistic bodywork practitioner will work on your emotional and energetic bodies as much as your physical, using various modes of touch (acupressure, massage and/or craniosacral, to name a few) teamed with intuitive healing and energy work to bring your body back to a place of rest, release and relief. I have not met anyone like Asha. Her sessions are some of the most beautiful and deeply nourishing somatic experiences I have ever had. On her massage table over the years, I have released much through my body – through crying, sounding, shaking and even feeling my soul travel to astral realms – while she has worked on me. I always leave feeling more 'in' my body, and like I have experienced an energetic breakthrough. The best way I can describe her work is that she heals.

On this particular day, I had recently received test results that my thyroid wasn't happy, my adrenals were running on empty and my cortisol was through the roof. I knew I needed an extra-long session to recalibrate my nervous system. But when Asha asked me what I wanted to work on that day, the tears popped up involuntarily as I sobbed, 'I just want to be done with this fear. I don't want to feel scared anymore.'

I had just received an aggressive text message, which had activated a whole heap of trauma in me (to the point where, if you know me, you know I rarely make or take phone calls as they are a huge trigger).

As I sobbed on her couch, Asha asked me a simple question. 'After this session, what would you like to feel?'

Without hesitation, I replied, 'Lighter.'

I lay face-down on her table and she got to work. It was one of those sessions where I completely disconnected from my body – and two hours flew by as if they were ten minutes. I could hardly believe it when I heard her whispering in my ear that it was time to come back into my body.

As we sat and debriefed, I felt noticeably different. My voice had dropped, my body felt relaxed and I felt so at-ease that I found it hard to even pay attention to what Asha was sharing with me.

'We cleared a lot of that fear from your solar plexus,' she shared. 'I was guided by your inner child – she was about 16 – and she showed me everywhere the energy needed to be released from.'

This made sense – my adolescence was a huge time of wounding for me, and much of those years were me wearing a mask and keeping everything inside.

She finished with, 'That was a really big session, Holl. It was a huge release. Go straight home and get some rest.'

I slowly walked to my car and was about to take the 30-minute drive back home, when I thought it might be good to stop into the IGA and grab something for dinner (a mum's job is never done). I was walking through the aisles with an empty basket when I first started to notice a subtle rumbling in my stomach. It was enough to stop me in my tracks – it came on out of nowhere – but I put it down to a little energy shift and didn't think much of it.

As I started piling groceries into my basket, the rumbling began to build. I started to feel sweaty, hot and lightheaded. There was no denying it – I needed a toilet immediately.

I rushed to the checkout, trying my hardest to play it cool while frantically calculating the closest public toilet. As the woman at the counter was scanning my dinner, I was nodding along with a smile to her small talk, all the while clenching so hard and fighting the urge to run right there, leaving my ingredients behind.

I needed to go. And I needed to go now.

I paid for my groceries, grabbed the bags and bolted to my car. There was a public toilet literally across the street. It would take 30 seconds to drive to. I was in the clear.

I sat down in the driver's seat, put on my seatbelt and … it happened.

No one ever tells you that when you shit yourself in a public place, a huge level of dissociation takes over. I left my body. I was genuinely watching this all unfold above me. And there was nothing I could do but wait for it to be over.

Now, I know what you're thinking – everyone shits themselves. It's fine. We're human.

But I need to make this clear – and then I promise, I will never bring it up again. When I mentioned to Asha I wanted to feel 'lighter', I did not think that would be a release of LITRES of shit. I'm not exaggerating – I mean, without measuring it, obviously – this release was violent, and it was EVERYWHERE. There was nothing I could do but wait for it to stop. And to paint a prettier picture for you – it was broad daylight. I was parked outside in a very busy, very public car park. I was wearing a dress. People were walking past me with their groceries, none the wiser that I was literally sitting in my own shit.

What followed was a frantic call to Trent (who thought the whole thing was hilarious) followed by a second frantic call to Asha (who was much more concerned). We decided that I would drive back to her workspace, and she would leave towels out for me to shower once her next client was settled in. In the meantime, mum-life meant I had a brand-new packet of wet wipes just begging to be used, and I just so happened to have some spare clothes in the back seat after a recent theatre performance, so I got busy cleaning myself – and the car – as best I could.

Now, the moral of this story is not that you will shit yourself after a bodywork session. I can almost (*almost*) guarantee that you won't. I have spoken to multiple bodywork practitioners since this experience, and none of them have heard of an experience like mine, Asha included. Bodywork is notoriously gentle. However – and I have been told this by countless practitioners I have seen through the years – my own body LOVES a somatic release. It moves things very quickly. I've had everyone from kinesiologists to chiropractors to somatic therapists tell me this. I'm a rare breed. And sometimes, it ends in public defecation.

So, why this story?

Because it's an example of what your body is holding onto, often without you even knowing it. And until we bring conscious intention, and a safe means of releasing to move it through, your body will continue to hold onto it. For me, I claimed I was done with the fear. I wanted to feel lighter. And I felt safe enough, being held by Asha, that I could really 'let go'. Not just metaphorically either. I fully and finally released. The fear that was backed up in my physical body meant that I couldn't properly release. This explains why even after 40 hours of labour I hadn't dilated to 10cm, why I tried pushing with my little girl for three and a half hours, breaking blood vessels in my eyes, to no avail. Even why it has always taken a long time for me to feel relaxed, open and ready for sexual penetration. To relax, to open, to soften has been a near impossible task my entire life because decades of accumulated fear left me tense, rigid and tight. And my physical body was holding all of that.

Even more fascinating is after this experience, I rabbit-holed down the phrase commonly used when we're afraid: 'I shat myself' or 'I was shitting myself'. I wanted to know why this was. And what I uncovered is it is a saying connected to the tension our sphincter holds when we are in a terror response. It only releases (and therefore lets our bowels flow) when we feel safe.

This somatic session activated safety in my system. My body released decades upon decades of built-up fear and tension. And the result was me violently shitting myself in my car. But for you, maybe it will look like a big emotional release – guttural sobs that can't be placed, an angry outburst, shaking up and down your body.

The body knows how to release when it's given a safe environment to do so. But how many of us are carving out the space and time to do this?

Sometimes I need to be reminded that I live on the Northern Rivers of New South Wales, and so practitioners that specialise in energetic healing and bodywork, for me, are relatively easy to come by. I know this isn't the case for everyone. With any practitioner that works in the energetic realms, recommendations and testimonials are a must. If someone you trust trusts a practitioner, that is usually a good sign that they know what they're doing. Old-school word-of-mouth marketing trumps any Google search or social clout these days, especially in the world of energy work. Start to ask around. Head along to a retreat that specialises in this type of work. Connect with people in your area online, who share the practitioners they see. And the right one, at the right time, will always show up for you.

Tremor/trauma release exercises (TRE)

I first experienced tremor releasing only recently in a therapy session. I had booked with a new therapist in my first year of postpartum healing back when I noticed I had some unprocessed rage that wanted to move through my body. This therapist came highly recommended to me as not only was she a qualified trauma-informed therapist, but she specialised in somatic healing and something known as family constellation work. The only exposure I'd had previously to this line of therapy was one of the Goop episodes on Netflix, but the premise of the practice made sense to me – that often the patterns, emotions and physical manifestations we experience can actually be inherited from our parents, or their parents or theirs. Family constellation work is the means of handing these patterns back to our ancestors and cutting the cord (so to speak) so that we don't have to carry anything that is not ours.

Our first few sessions together were pretty straightforward. I shared my entire family history, including that of my parents, and what I knew of their parents – from physical health, to mental health, to careers, positions in family trees, you name it, she knew it. She drew up this incredible constellation connecting the dots between all of my family members and leaving me as the starting point. And then we would speak (like traditional talk therapy) about what I was personally experiencing. We would move into a meditative practice that would guide me to a particular family member who held the 'root' of the emotion I was experiencing. The anxiety I was carrying about men being unsafe? That actually didn't belong to me, and I could hand it back to my grandmother. The unprocessed rage I was feeling that just needed somewhere to go? It was time to give that back to my nannu.

The sessions were powerful in their subtlety and after three I was already noticing a difference in the intensity of what I had been feeling.

And then I decided to book one more session to work on a particular issue that was causing me grief. My little girl has never been easy in the car. To this day, she will vomit on car trips, and now that she is able to use her voice, she tells me it is because she feels 'stuck' in her car seat. I am aware enough to know that this is her body communicating something and the vomit is her way of releasing. That her feeling of stuckness likely points to her feeling of stuckness in her birth. Because … well, she WAS stuck. She was so stuck that we needed forceps to get her out. And so her little system is doing what it knows best: using that feeling of stuckness to move energy that's ready to be released.

The only thing is I've had a vomit-phobia for as long as I can remember. Give me mass defecation any day over a vomit sesh. I literally recoil in fear. And so I figured, why not work on this one with my therapist? It worked on everything else, surely it would on this?

I explained the history of my phobia, how I had to work on it because my little girl seemed to be a 'vomiter' and I didn't want to be in terror every time we went for a drive. We traced the phobia back to a family member who also had this phobia, and started to hand the fear back to them. As we were doing this, I felt my right hand start to shake. It was subtle, but enough for her to notice over the Zoom call.

'Hollie, can you exaggerate the shaking in your right hand a little for me, please?' she asked.

I thought that was a bit odd, but trusted her, so started to exaggerate the movements a little bigger. Before I knew what was happening, the shaking took over both hands, both arms and worked its way up my entire body until it reached my face. I wasn't scared – I had my therapist guiding me the whole time, letting me know this was tremor releasing and my body was ready to let go of some deep trauma, that this is what animals do naturally when they are in fear, that we just haven't given our bodies safe enough spaces to process in this way. I spent most of the session in a tremor release. It moved through my limbs, my face contorting outside of my own control, my mouth twitching. It was incredible. I had no idea my body could do this! It was moving so fast, outside of any conscious control. And all I had done was bring intention to what I wanted to release paired with a space that felt safe enough for me to let go.

I have experienced tremor releasing multiple times now. My most extreme was while sitting a half-day shadow healing, where I had set the intention to release my fear of men once and for all. I shook on the couch for hours, but only up my right side (uncoincidentally, my 'masculine side') while my left remained incredibly still. The energy that moved out of me was some of the most intense energy healing I have ever felt.

When we experience a tremor release, our bodies use shaking or vibrating to release muscular tension, burn excess adrenaline and calm the nervous system to its neutral state, thereby managing stress levels.[33] Tremor release therapy is another means of nervous system regulation, a deep somatic practice that connects us back with our natural biological response when we feel fear or terror.

So, can we do this at home?

This is best practised to begin with under the guidance of a trauma-informed somatic therapist who specialises in TRE. However, over time, once the practices are learned, you can do them at home. They are particularly beneficial to anyone experiencing PTSD, anxiety, trauma or chronic stress.

For me? I find my body will move stress and trauma through tremor releasing of its own accord. These days, I don't even need to use the exercises to bring them on (although again, I have a very sensitive system!).

A simple start point is to shake your hands out any time you feel overwhelmed by stress or energy you want to release. Imagine

33 www.healthline.com/health/mental-health/can-shaking-your-body-heal-stress-and-trauma#How-to-do-it

as you are shaking your hands that you are also releasing any energy that is not yours to carry. You will likely feel even a subtle lightness in this simple practice.

Energetic burnout

I was getting ready to head to my chiro appointment when I was overcome by a wave of what I can only describe as displaced energy. That is, energy that came out of nowhere, that didn't feel like my own.

I found myself feeling very hot, very quickly, and when I checked my Whoop data, my heartrate had jumped to 110 bpm. I took a moment to stop and feel what was happening. Where did this come from? I knew that I could eliminate a hypoglycemic episode as I had just eaten a well-rounded meal (thanks, Chantel!) and I'd also just had a solid nap, so I was well-rested. My health metrics have only been on the up since implementing all of the practices I've shared in Chapter 5. My stress monitor was stable. What was going on?

And then it dawned on me. Could this be energetic?

I sat in my car and cleared my energy with the practices I have in my energetic toolkit. I called in my guides, called my energy back to me, and released anything I was unnecessarily carrying that was not mine. The relief was almost instant. I could literally feel my own energy return to my body, which only amplified following my chiropractic appointment. I literally felt more myself.

It got me thinking. If my own body was reacting in this instance to an energy that I had randomly picked up on going about my normal stay-at-home-mum day, impacting my body to the point of temperature change and increase in heart rate, then how many of us are going around experiencing the same, with no idea what to do with it?

This led me down a trail of other questions:

Does everyone experience energetic hooks like this, or only those more 'tapped in'?

What does the everyday person do when they experience something like this, with no idea what it is or how to clear it?

And, most importantly:

How can we establish a relationship with our energetic wellbeing that is spoken about – and valued as highly – as that of our physical wellbeing?

We've got a long way to go when it comes to truly understanding and respecting the nature of our whole human selves being so much more than our physical vessels. And don't get me wrong – our bodies are so important. Without them, we literally don't get to live, so I'm not discrediting them for a second. I like living. Living can stay.

But what is missing, especially in today's mass societal rhetoric that favours science over what can't be typically explained by a research paper, is even a baseline understanding of ourselves as energetic beings, and what this means for us. Whether you're a reiki healer, a psychic medium or a GP, we are all energetic beings with energetic bodies that are in constant communication with us, desiring to be looked after.

And it is vital that we tend to these parts of ourselves as often as we are booking our blood tests, nourishing our bodies with wholefoods, moving regularly and ensuring we get adequate sleep and solid hydration.

Something interesting happened to me at the beginning of the year. After re-opening my psychic reading books in new motherhood to a sold-out waitlist, ongoing bookings and being the leading source of income in my return to work for two solid years, my intuition guided me to close my books. That is, no more readings, indefinitely.

At this time, I hadn't yet signed a book deal, my new model management wasn't on the cards and did I mention I had a huge waitlist of clients and this was my sole income stream? But something told me it was time to take a break. And I trusted it, like all matters of my intuition.

A number of things happened following the closing of my psychic readings.

The week following, I was approached by my publishers to sign book deal two (thanks, guys!). The same week of signing this deal, I also signed on with my new modelling management team. And to top it off, I landed the lead understudy role for my local theatre production.

Life was ticking away beautifully, slotting comfortably in the new space I had created for it. But that wasn't even the biggest piece. The biggest piece, that I am only realising now, is that alongside all of this creative success, my health started to take a rapid decline. Following putting my sessions on hold, I was no longer dropping into someone else's energy for 45 minutes at a time. And while to this day I LOVE to do this work, I know now that my body was telling me it was time for a break. My body couldn't hold anyone else's energy anymore – it could barely hold my own.

This isn't the first time I've experienced a form of burnout. My first ever experience of adrenal fatigue was in corporate land, which made clear-as-anything sense to me: I didn't enjoy my job, I was commuting hours at a time daily, working around the clock and not feeling fulfilled in most areas of my life. It was a recipe for burnout.

My first big burnout when I was working for myself landed at a time I was seeing up to 12 clients a week for readings. That made sense – it was too much energy for me to hold, so I scaled back to only two readings a week.

Then I started experiencing another bout of burnout even in only seeing two clients a week, as I had started weaving mediumship (connecting with spirits who have crossed over) into my sessions. This flavour of burnout, at its worst, had me injecting vitamin B12 into my legs to get through a day.

Fast-forward to now. While life is on the up in so many ways, my health is on the down. And a major throughline I can see is that it started when I picked up my readings again.

What I've found most difficult to come to terms with is when my body is unable to hold the work that brings me joy. But what I'm only noticing now is that it's specifically the energetic work that brings me joy.

Writing doesn't burn me out. Performing doesn't burn me out. Modelling doesn't burn me out. But energetic work does. Readings and healings and channelling for other people.

And as someone navigating this season of my life with health that needs to be prioritised, it's taken a lot for me to realise that saying yes to me might look like saying no to things I really, truly love and believe in. It looks like choosing me above anyone or anything else.

You are likely not an intuitive reader or a psychic or an astrologer or a healer (but respect, if you are). It doesn't matter, because you ARE an energetic being. And you are an energetic being interacting with other energetic beings every single day. And if I can become burned out doing ALL of the 'right things' when it comes to holding my own energetic boundaries even when tuning into someone else's energy field, then you bet that you can also be picking up on other people's energetic stuff and be none the wiser. Especially if you don't have ongoing energetic practices for your own wellbeing. Your Whoop can't track this stuff. Energy is unseen and so deeply misunderstood, and so, for the most part, it is ignored. Which isn't doing our health any favours.

I decided to see if I could uncover anything that specifically draws the line between people who work in spiritual or energetic faculties, and their relationship with chronic illness and/or burnout. Because this throughline made sense to me, not just in my own experience, but in the experiences of countless colleagues and friends who work in some form of healing modality, and most of whom experience chronic stress, illness, burnout and/or autoimmune conditions. I wanted to give science the benefit of the doubt here; however, as expected, it appears this category of work has not been looked into yet.

What I did find in my searching was a multitude of research papers referencing 'healing the healer' in the context of medical healing: doctors, nurses and carers in the health space. The research was astounding.

In the US, suicide deaths are 250–400 per cent higher among female physicians when compared to women in other professions.[34] The term 'spiritual burnout' has even been coined by Christian healthcare missionaries, pointing to the intense emotional drain involved with seeing patients.[35] The closest thread I found to research in support of spiritual workers and burnout is actually a paper that concludes that having a daily spiritual practice is an evidenced burnout preventative.[36] While the research isn't direct, it is still clear in many facets; namely, that spiritual practices are a vital component of ensuring wellbeing in healthcare workers who are experiencing burnout.

And for the purposes of this book, I am going to be so bold as to categorise any person who works on the healing of another (be it physical healing, energetic healing or spiritual healing) as a healthcare worker. Because the stressors remain the same. The pressure remains the same. The holding of someone's energy is some of the most intense work you can do. And that's not just if you consciously are doing it. If you're moving through life as an open energetic sponge, then chances are you're unknowingly holding a heap of energy that isn't yours.

34 www.psychologytoday.com/au/blog/healing-the-wounded-healers/202204/healing-the-wounded-healers
35 www.medicalmissions.com/resources/25145/spiritual-burnout
36 pubmed.ncbi.nlm.nih.gov/26549835

So, how do we move it? How do we know when we've picked up on energy that isn't ours, and what do we do to ensure our energetic bodies remain solid and intact?

First, it's vital you have a sense of what your own energy feels like, without any outside influence or interference. This is key because once you have an understanding of your own energy, you'll also have an understanding of what isn't your energy. I sort of liken it to your own unique style – you know when you try on a piece of clothing that just isn't you? Like the time I took my fitspo-loving friend Katie into Tree of Life and begged her to try on a pink floral dress. It wasn't going to happen, because it isn't her.

Same goes here. We want to get so incredibly clear on what is and isn't ours, energetically speaking, that as soon as we pick something up that isn't, we're aware of it.

This is where modalities like human design (a system used to explain your unique energetic and life blueprint) and astrology are exceptionally helpful in gauging an understanding of our energy, and how we uniquely thrive, versus how society reflects we 'should' thrive. These modalities are rooted in ancient practices used over hundreds and thousands of years – there's nothing new (age) about them. And despite the people in your life sharing that 'studies have found people who believe in astrology are more likely to be narcissists' (eye roll), there *is* validity in using these modalities as reference points to gauge a more thorough understanding of yourself as people have been doing for millennia.

As a practising astrologer, every reading I have ever given has been met with an exhale, because the person I am reading for has finally been given permission to be more of who they really are. More uniquely them. More in their own energy. And when we have this permission, we are able to lean on this deeper understanding of ourselves and use it as a benchmark for what we say yes to, what we say no to, when we are living in our highest expression, the things that make us shine and often where we have blind spots that require a little more work.

A beautiful example of this is when I first uncovered that I was a 'projector' in human design. This was the first time in my life I was given an explanation as to why, no matter how hard I tried to fit into the standard 9–5 working life, I just couldn't do it. And not because I didn't like to work hard – far from it! – but because no matter what I tried, my energy just couldn't keep up. Uncovering my human design gave me permission to take my energy seriously, in all its uniqueness. That I'm here to lead and to work in a different way and to share my voice as I figure life out (I am a 3/5 self-projected projector, for those playing along).

The same thing happened when I had my astrology chart read for the very first time. I wasn't just a Leo anymore; I was actually so much Virgo – my Venus, Mars and Mercury. I had a Libra Moon, which explained my love of beauty and my exceptional 'skill' at wearing masks and putting everyone before myself. Having my chart read illuminated shadows of mine I never thought could ever come up in an astrology reading, including childhood behaviours, family dynamics and pieces of myself I had never spoken aloud.

These modalities are allies when used to enhance our understanding of ourselves, and therefore enhance our quality of life. They are not designed to be used as cop-outs or excuses for poor behaviour. They are an invitation into our edges – to look at the aspects of ourselves that are desirable, yes, but also challenging. And when we have this level of self-awareness, we are able to live life in a more informed way.

I spoke to Amy Lea, popular human design and astrology reader and teacher, about how these modalities aid in us living from a place of energetic integrity, authenticity and truth. She says:

> This is possibly the most important and impactful thing about human design and astrology, that they are all about self-understanding and self-awareness. I often hear from people who look at these modalities from the outside and think that they are putting themselves into boxes, but when you dive in you realise pretty quickly that these systems actually help us move beyond boxes and labels. They are ultimately systems of liberation, designed to help us see all of the identities and stories that the world has conditioned us to take on, all of the ways we have been living for others, and all of the ways we have been repressing or denying our own truth.
>
> And it's through seeing all of this, that we can begin to uncover who we really are and start allowing our true self to emerge. Both of these modalities are designed to help us see how we are unique, multidimensional beings with millions of traits and layers that make us wholly unique.

So rather than wearing the identity of 'I'm a Leo' (which lacks any nuance, and is absolutely placing yourself in a pop-culture-generated tick-box of likely funny but also painfully constricting memes), when used as intended, these modalities allow you to understand the depth and richness of why you are the way you are.

When it comes to people abdicating their own authority or power to these modalities, Amy believes that it is vital we become aware of our own unique authority. That way, in any reading – be it astrological, human design or even psychic – we can take what resonates, and leave the rest. This isn't about bending to the teachings; it is about using them to enhance our understanding of who we are.

Once you have a more thorough understanding of your unique energetic signature – and what you need (and do not need) to thrive – you've reached the next stage of tuning in. That is, your own personal energetic maintenance practices that do not require a practitioner to ensure that, no matter what you pick up on as you go about your days, you are able to come back to a centred, grounded and embodied state.

These practices are all primary tools I used as a psychic reader when I was tuning into the energy of other people regularly; however, they can also be used by anyone wanting to tend to their energy field a little more lovingly (and surely you know by now, this should be all of us?).

Setting energetic boundaries

To be clear: it's one thing (and important!) to use the block, mute and unfollow buttons, set up your automated out-of-office email, put your phone on flight mode, or even end a friendship. It's another thing entirely to anchor into your own energy each day.

A simple way to do this is by 'calling back all parts of you'. You can do this at the end of your day, or even any time throughout the day you feel rattled by someone else's energy. My favourite time to do this is in the shower at the end of the day.

Close your eyes, place a hand or two on your heart, and repeat internally or aloud: 'I call all parts of me back to my body, and release any energy that is not mine.'

Repeat this as often as you feel comfortable – you can even repeat your name aloud if that feels right. As you repeat the sentence, imagine any energy that is yours flooding back into your body as you breathe in, and any energy that isn't yours flooding out of your body as you breathe out. This might feel like a weight has been lifted from your shoulders – even subtly. It could feel like energy buzzing or tingling in your hands, and you may even find yourself needing to take a big sigh. These are all beautiful signs that you are shifting energy. I like to shake my hands at the end of the practice to move anything 'sticky' out. And yep, you might cringe the first time you try this, but I bet after a week or two, you're going to feel better than ever.

Here is another beautiful practice you can use at the start of your day, if you know you are heading into a space that may feel a little more energetically 'taxing' than you'd like. This could be a family event that may have some tension, or even the buzz of a big shopping centre. Before you head out to the event or outing, imagine you are 'pulling in' your energy as if you were putting on a big jacket. I like to practise this in the shower at the beginning of the day, but you could even do this in the car or a public toilet space. Take a few deep breaths and imagine that as you 'pull on' your energetic jacket, you are protected in a bubble of white light. You might visualise this in your mind's eye, or maybe it's simply a sensation you feel. Just as you wouldn't head into a blizzard without your coat, imagine the same goes when you're stepping into any environment that has the potential for intense energetic overload. Pop on your energetic coat.

Salt water

Salt water is a huge energy transmuter and something I was consistently taught to harness by mentors when I was training as a psychic, and especially in mediumship training (you can imagine the types of energy I was picking up on back then). Salt water is a known energy cleanser and cleanses your auric field, which is why we feel so good after an ocean swim.

If you can't jump into the ocean regularly, using a salt scrub in the shower, or bath salts in your bath, is key. This is especially vital for anyone with strong Pisces placements (Sun, Moon, Rising), or anyone who considers themselves an empath. Salt water will transmute the energy you pick up through your day. Use it every day if you can.

When I need to shift particularly heavy energy from my day – or even if I need to cultivate a deep state of rest – I will be sure to use salt water in some way. That way I know I have my entire energetic body online, and I am not connected to anyone else's. A bath with salts, 528hz music and some gentle breathwork is energetic medicine.

Washing hands

Another easy one to remember – and something I did after every psychic reading I held (of which there have been thousands) – is washing your hands. Again, water is a beautiful transmuter of energy, and our hands are a direct link to our heart spaces (our hands grew from our hearts when we were little embryos. Isn't that cute?).

When you're washing your hands, close your eyes and imagine your energy flooding back to you. Do this any time you feel you've picked up on anything particularly dense or heavy. It can particularly be a good practice to lean on if you work in an office or corporate environment.

Connection with your guides and spirit team

One of the biggest questions I receive is *how do I connect with my guides?* This topic is a book in itself, so I will keep the answer succinct and clear here, knowing that this is simply gently stepping into this world (and there are beautiful practitioners and readers available if you'd like to dive deeper).

A wonderful starting point in connecting with your spirit team (made up of your own spirit guides, guardian angels and ancestors and loved ones who have passed) is to start a line of communication with them. Pray. Speak to them. Ask for their wisdom. Ask for guidance. Ask for signs. When you see angel numbers like 11:11, smile up at your guides (I always look up at least) and thank them for their guidance. When you find a feather, when a song repeatedly plays that holds the answer to a question you were grappling with, when something you're reading takes your breath away because of how relevant it is to you and your life right now – look up and say thank you.

This open line of communication is one of the clearest and most rewarding places to start. You don't need to know the specifics of who you're talking to (I find that often we get so caught up in 'who' they are, we miss the point entirely – which is, what they're here to offer us). Your guidance team exists for exactly that – to guide you. But how can they guide you if you're not asking for guidance?

Write your questions down, write *what do my guides have to tell me?*, sit quietly and let them answer through your pen (this is often referred to as 'free writing'). Put on some 528hz music, close your eyes, place your hand on your heart and invite them into your room – feel the energy shift when they arrive. Before you go to sleep at night, welcome in your guides and ask them to answer any questions you might have in your dreams.

The biggest piece here is to just start connecting with them. Get out of your head and don't get caught up in the need to know exactly who they are and why they're your guide (this is often just our ego wanting a cool story to tell, which is not the point).

Ask, and you shall receive.

A beautiful guide to call in, who is available for any of us in any moment, is Archangel Michael. A guardian angel of the highest light, we can call on him any time we need energetic protection or healing. When I was praying to the 'powers that be' last week for my healing, I was calling on Archangel Michael regularly. You can call on him when you're driving, travelling or before sleep for uninterrupted rest.

Always offer your thanks when you do this – just like any relationship, our guides are deserving of gratitude and thanks for all they do for us too.

Embodiment practices / ecstatic movement

Not dissimilar to tremor releasing, a beautiful and easy somatic practice to move unwanted energy and come back to the heart of our own feelings and experiences lies in ecstatic movement. That is, moving your body freely, without thought, in a way that promotes feelings of ecstasy.

Reserve your judgement (and panic) here: there is no need for anyone to witness your moves if that isn't your thing. What lies at the core of this practice is simply free movement. No one needs to know, and no one needs to see.

I find when I intentionally practise ecstatic movement, I am always drawn to moving my hips – gentle rocking, turning into giant swaying and circular motions. This makes sense because I also know our hip flexors store much unprocessed anger (which I seem to have an issue with, if that hasn't become obvious). Moving my hips for five minutes – to my own music, in my own room, in my own time – has unlocked so much in me. I can start by dancing and end in crying, yelling (into my pillow), or even bigger movements of my body, like stomping my feet, swinging my arms, shaking my head and even sometimes tremor releasing.

If we think of emotion as 'energy in motion', what happens when that energy has nowhere to go? We unlock it, through motion. Movement. It doesn't have to be dance. Yoga is beautiful for this too. Going for a sweaty run could be your movement of choice. But I do believe there is an important part of this practice that lies in the free embodiment of our sensual selves, an unlocking which releases a raw, primal and powerful nature, especially in those of us who have been shamed for these parts of ourselves.

Ecstatic dance is a beautiful embodiment practice to bring your energy back into your body while also liberating you from societal conditioning that has wronged you for your body in the first place.

Vocal toning

While I'm not suggesting musical theatre as an energetic healer (actually, I am – see Chapter 7), the natural partner to embodied dance is embodied voice. Or, its technical term, vocal toning. This practice of using the voice to move and heal energy (using a range of sounds, from singing and humming to deep audible sighing) has even been scientifically evidenced to result in 'meditative, calm and relaxed' experiences.[37] There is a reason song bathing and crystal singing bowls are modes of energetic activation and healing. An extension of what we know about music is simply this: sound heals. And using your own voice and sounds has a significant impact on your own energy, and your own somatic releasing.

Like much energy work, the key lies in not overthinking it.

Carve aside space and time to move energy through your voice in whatever way feels true to you. It could be taking a deep breath in, and audibly sighing out – as loud as you can, until you feel emptied of sound and energy. It could be humming in your own rhythm, allowing the energy of your voice to guide you to the notes. Or maybe you're a little more extreme, like me, and prefer a giant yell into a pillow when energy feels pent up.

My little girl has just started singing in the shower – it is the sweetest thing, and so natural in her (this has all been of her own

37 pubmed.ncbi.nlm.nih.gov/29800304

accord). While I know many of us enjoying a good shower-sing sesh are likely doing it because of the acoustics, I do wonder if there is something energetic in it too – being alone, in the water, allowing energy to move through us at the end of the day.

When starting out, there is no wrong way. The key is to find a way to let that energy move through you, specifically through your voice.

Scent

Scent is my thing. I joke to Trent about my 'supersonic sense of smell'. So of course it was another permission slip when I discovered my cognition in human design (pointing to our strongest sense) is smell. But it's not just a thing for us super-smellers; scent is a beautiful tool to use as an anchor, and to bring your energy back to the present moment.

Earthy scents like frankincense, sandalwood, vetiver and cedarwood are all powerful in activating states of 'grounding', increasing feelings of relaxation and even supporting sleep. From a spiritual perspective, these oils are sacred in their ability to heal and calm (there's a reason frankincense is said to have been one of the gifts given to baby Jesus). Placing a drop or two of your woody oil of choice on your feet, or in your bath, is a beautiful way to anchor your energy back into your body and ground you in the here and now.

If oils aren't your thing, incense or scented mists are other beautiful ways to use scent as an anchor of energetic protection. Lighting incense in your space, or spritzing a mist after a particularly heavy day, not only cultivates beauty (which we know now is calming to our nervous systems) but also creates a calmer environment for your energetic body as well. This is why any time you visit any sort of energy practitioner, their space smells beautiful. They know how to use scent as an anchor for healing, and energetic wellbeing.

Find a scent that works for you – like your signature scent, but for your energetic body rather than your physical body. One that feels like home. Use it in your mists, grab it in incense form, diffuse it in your home, or dab it straight on your wrists when you're needing to come 'back' into your body.

If you're looking for grounding energy, think oils from the earth like sandalwood, cedarwood, anything 'wood' really. Citrus notes (like lemon and orange) are regularly used as uplifting, positive scents, while florals will aid in dropping into a receptive, flowing and soft energy.

Ritual space

The beauty of having a go-to ritual for your energy body is that you don't have to overthink it. It's as simple as taking what is listed above and making it your own. Something I will say though, is it is special to have a space in your home dedicated to your energy practices and rituals. While sometimes this will take place in a bathtub (like me last night – I went all out with rose petals, oils, salts; the works!) – there is something special about having a dedicated space to come back to your energy. It's like an exhale for your energetic body. I'm lucky enough to have an entire room for this (it's where I write from) and any time I have a friend over to sit in my room with a cacao, they comment on the energy in the space. Nothing compares, because it is dedicated to uplifting my energy. And so, the space is a highly concentrated indication of that.

For you, it could be as simple as setting up an altar, a special corner in your home with your beautiful objects that bring you back to your energy – think scented sprays, oils, oracle decks, crystals, your vision board and any objects that inspire and uplift your energy field. I always have fresh flowers on my altar, as well as incense and some rosemary for smoke-smudging. Try not to overcomplicate it.

Over time, this altar will start to hold the purest vibrations of your own energy – and so, when you sit in your ritual, be it a cacao ritual, a yoga nidra practice, an EFT sesh or a good old scream in the pillow, you will feel deeply grounded in your own energy, during and after. Sometimes when I'm short on time, I'll simply walk into my room, take a deep breath in, glance at my vision board and leave. It can literally be that simple.

Ritual also lies in the frequency of sitting a practice. Whatever it is, make a commitment to showing up frequently for your energy body. Whatever frequent is to you – maybe you only have five minutes each evening before bed, where you spritz your mist and sit in quiet contemplation and journalling. Maybe you can commit to an hour-long ceremony every week. Be realistic, but also – show up. This is the sacred part of you that longs to be activated and is, more often than not, the very first thing to be forgotten or neglected. And in doing so, our energetic body gets left behind. Remember that on our journey to say yes to ourselves – this means saying yes to ALL of us. Our physical AND our energetic bodies. They both matter. And so showing up for both matters too.

ACTIVITY: **Creating your altar**

Below are some key points to consider when setting up your altar. Remember, this doesn't have to be an entire room; it could simply be a corner of your bedroom, or the windowsill in your favourite nook at home.

- Consider the location of your altar. Is there a vantage point in your home that provides an outlook of a beautiful sunrise or sunset? Can you set your altar up so that you're looking out at a beautiful tree in your garden? Trying to incorporate nature into your sacred space is not to be underrated – the energy of your view and how it makes you feel when sitting in the space will create ripples from the outside in.

- Pay attention to what furniture you are drawn to when creating your altar. Are you setting it up on a sideboard table (like the rose quartz one I found on marketplace? #win!), or do you have a really cute shelving unit from Kmart? Maybe your altar space is set on your office desk. Or your bookshelf. Or a tiny table you found in an antique store. Do you have plush cushions to sit on and meditate by your altar, or will you be using your office chair? Get clear on where is best for you to set up, knowing that your sacred space can offer a moment of ritual anywhere, at any time.

- I had a friend visit recently who remarked when looking at my altar space, 'Gosh, this is just so you. It's beautiful, and colourful, and I instantly think of you when I see it.' This is the point – your altar is yours. What feels sacred, special or beautiful to you will be different to your best friend, sister or partner. For me, it looks like a couple of pieces from my favourite local artist, fresh flowers (I buy them every week because #beauty) and my favourite crystals. As I mentioned earlier, my vision board also lives here, alongside some candles and incense. For you, your altar might be barer than mine. Maybe you have a really special object handed down to you from a family member. Maybe you have framed photos of loved ones who have passed. Whatever feels sacred and special to you is the point.

- I like to use smoke to bless my altar every week. Like a cleansing for any other sacred space, I'm thanking my altar for the energies it offers me through the week and inviting in energies of the highest light. These spaces can become highly concentrated over time, so tending to the energy of the space is key to you continuing to reap the benefits.

Tune in

When I recently found myself neglecting the energetic practices I have just shared, following my big health flare-up, I knew without question what I needed to do. I had slowed my system down enough, but now it was time to tune in. I asked my beautiful friend, kinesiologist and author of *Change Your Life*,

Zoe Bosco, to come and help me get to the 'energetic roots' of what was happening physically in my body.

Zoe and I often use one another as sounding-boards for energetic clarity when we are moving through something big – physically, emotionally or otherwise. We often laugh that people would be shocked at the weird and wonderful rituals and magic energy practices we use on one another to move energy. In the spirit of transparency, it's so important that we no longer dilute or hide our weird, wonderful magic sides, because what lies in these practices is the root of the healing that I know so many of us are seeking.

Zoe came right over and I explained what I had been realising: that while I had been tackling my physical health head-on – tracking my data, taking all of the supplements, adjusting my food and sleep and movement, doing all of the things – I'd realised there was a missing link: the energetic cause behind all of this. If it were an equation it would look like this: *physical root cause + energetic root cause = true healing.*

We knew my physical body was experiencing hypothyroidism, mast-cell activation syndrome, chronic stress and adrenal burnout, not to mention a number of gut dysbiosis and nutrient deficiencies. We knew that this was likely linked to the traumatic childhood I experienced, and the compounded trauma in my system that reached overflow when I became a mother. What we hadn't pinpointed – yet – was the true energetic undercurrent of these pieces. What energy wanted to be healed? And how?

Zoe quickly 'tuned into my field'. When I say that, what I mean was she used her own energy field to pick up on mine. When energy workers do this, they become one with your own energetic body, which enables them to 'read' what is occurring in your system. You may have experienced this through reiki or a muscle-testing practice like kinesiology. Zoe uses her own extremely powerful and unique way of tuning in, and then provides space for the healing of your vital energetic signs.

What came up for me was both unsurprising (but of course!) and mind-blowing. My system was testing as a fear-and-freeze response, related to the next life chapter I am currently stepping into. While signing this book deal, and signing with my new modelling management in the same week, looks (and feels) like huge creative success – and points to everything I have ever desired in my career coming to fruition – the reality is that my energetic body hadn't processed the gravity of these pieces.

More eyes on my work. More vulnerability in what I am sharing. The high likelihood of more people talking about me and judging me. My first time in front of a camera professionally since motherhood, and all that brings up for me in relationship to my body. The fear, the fear, the fear.

And this fear wasn't around failure; it was around success. What happens if this book is successful? What happens if I book a huge campaign and my body is plastered all over shopfront windows? Will I be able to hold that level of success?

Logically, it excites me. This is exactly what my vision board is reflecting back to me as I write. I truly, truly want this.

Energetically, my system was afraid.

And so we tuned into *why*. What was underneath this fear, this freeze, that was keeping me 'stuck' and 'small'? What was underneath my body, sending me all of the physical warning signs to slow down, to hide away, to do the exact opposite of what I truly desire?

In this case, what was holding me back were patterns from my childhood (they often lie here) where I was made to believe it was unsafe to be seen or to be heard. Where I was the constant object of 'joking' criticism for talking to boys and for the shape of my body – for the size of my breasts, for my curves, from as early as when I hit puberty at 12 years old. The compounding of this behaviour, these words, these aggressions, all directed at me led my system to believe – at an age of identity formation, no less – that it was unsafe to take up space, to be seen, to literally exist in a woman's body. That my life was the butt of a dangerous joke. And so, when we do not move this energy through, it stays stuck, dictating life experiences that perhaps aren't congruent with our true desires, but won't move unless we give the energy the possibility of moving.

My energetic body had been holding onto all of this fear so intently because nowhere had I told it that things have changed; that they are not my beliefs, that I am safe to fully and wholly take up space in the expression of my body.

So that is what we did. Together on my couch, Zoe and I cleared my entire energetic body. We cleared my chakras (no surprises it was my throat and solar plexus needing love here), we cleared my nervous system, we cleared every form of energy you could think of.

There were moments I had emotion arise as we cleared, and so I let myself fully feel the emotion. There were moments I needed to talk out what was arising – to share and be witnessed in my sharing (for which Zoe is brilliant). And there were moments that didn't have words or feelings, but moved through as bodily sensations – goosebumps, a need to shake my hands, heat moving through my system. I welcomed them all, knowing that this is how our bodies like to shift energy.

What came out of this clearing was a number of action steps I needed to take to communicate to my body that it was now safe to fully step into this next iteration of me. I needed to end projects that no longer aligned with the version of me I was stepping into. I needed to find ways to embody sensuality that felt safe and witnessed. I needed to listen to my energetic body as much as my physical.

And with this new intel, I am able to book my bodywork session with Asha with this in mind. I am able to pursue the energetic healing modalities that feel best for me right now as I work on this deep energetic healing (kinesiology, EFT and chiropractic care are my tools of choice right now). And in the spirit of expanding my window of tolerance (because our nervous systems respond to the energetic as much as the physical), I am currently playing with expansion in dynamics specifically related to taking up space in my body, and letting myself be seen in that regard. Wearing clothes that do not hide my shape. Sharing photos where I feel beautiful. And while I am nervous around what people might say, I share them nonetheless because I'm showing myself that it's okay.

That I'm safe now.

That it's my birthright to shine.

And guess what?

It's yours too.

CHAPTER 7

Shine Bright

We said goodbye to our dog, Archie, yesterday. It seems like a cruel irony that my writing has been timed specifically on the section of the book about shining, literally the morning after we said our goodbyes. I am in the thick of grief – I can't remember the last time I cried so hard, and so much. My heart aches and the house feels so empty without his energy. My little girl keeps asking, 'Where's Archie?' and just when I think my heart is hanging in there, it crumbles into a million pieces again.

Life as we know it will never be the same, without our little man. And yet, it also goes on.

Now, I could do what most of us do when faced with a deep emotional upheaval. Slap on the 'I'm okay' face, and soldier on with life, holding back the tears when they spring behind my eyes. Heck, I didn't even need to share this in my writing. I could have just swallowed it down and written something far easier for the sake of 'getting the job done'.

But then I'd be missing the entire point of this journey I've travelled while writing this book: to say yes to you is to say yes to ALL OF YOU. All parts of you. The messy and the magic. The light and the darkness.

And to shine bright – to emit your true, vibrant glow in the world – is to live with your heart at the forefront of everything you do.

And guess what? Our heart holds love, and light, absolutely. But it holds equal parts grief, and heartbreak. Joy lives in our heart, and so does loss.

We cannot possibly experience grief if we haven't experienced love. To open our hearts to love in all ways – living a life with love at the forefront – is to understand that grief will also come. But it's choosing love anyway.

Choosing to shine in your life is similar to this notion.

Because when choosing to shine – truly shine – we're also choosing our shadow. It's saying, 'I am choosing to be light in my life, knowing that the equal and opposite part of this is dark – and I will choose that when it comes too.'

This is the law of polarity. For everything in our world, there is an opposite. And in this case, when we shine, we will also experience darkness. You cannot possibly have one without the other.

And this is what people are craving. In an era of social media filters, mask-wearing has taken on a whole new level. Not only are we slapping on an 'I'm okay' face to our loved ones in real-time, but now we're doing it to the masses online as well. In an era of artificial intelligence, we're likely going to be exposed to more robotic energy than ever before – technology writing poetry, writing songs, creating art, taking photos. And what is going to set us apart is our substance. Our very human, very honest, very vulnerable souls.

When I shared earlier that postpartum was the hardest time of my life and I truly thought my life was over, I didn't do it because it felt easy to share; I shared it because that is the honest truth. Despite the vulnerability hangover that will likely come when this book is on shelves, that is the truth of my lived experience.

When I speak about my health challenges and how hard it has been, I'm not doing it to seek attention. I'm sharing it because if I avoid that truth, if I cut any corners to the truth of my story, then what I am telling myself (and in turn, telling you) is that those parts of me aren't wanted. They're not palatable enough. People will turn their heads away.

And you know what? They probably will. There will always be people not ready to hear the depths of your life – that's okay. Because I'm not sharing to be palatable or to uphold any ideals that are light and love only.

To shine brightly is to own all parts of your journey, your stories, your truth. It's to openly share when someone asks you how you are that it's been a hard time lately (if that is true). Just as it is celebrated to share when you're in the shine, it is so important we are witnessed in the shadow too.

When I started writing this book, at the very beginning, I was in a moment of real shine. After years of feeling lost and without a semblance of knowing what was next for me outside of motherhood, life felt like it was finally on my side. I had reason to celebrate. There was a noticeable spring in my step. I felt so, so proud, excited and happy. Truly happy.

The same week this all unfolded, a few things happened to friends in my life. One of my closest friends experienced a miscarriage. Another started a very challenging IVF journey that would also end in miscarriage. Another had just had a new baby and was in the hospital for some challenges with her little boy. And another was struggling with her own identity stepping into a new work role. All beautiful close friends of mine who were in it. They didn't feel shiny – far from it. They were in the polarity.

And I felt like shit. Because I felt guilty, and that it was unfair of me to hold my shine while they were all so clearly suffering.

I showed up for them as best I could during that time. I spent time with my friend who miscarried, taking her a heap of tinctures, herbs and food, holding her while she cried. I invited another to stay for the weekend to give her a break. I cooked her dinner and we spoke well into the night. I was on voice notes to another every day, and sent her flowers and I sent some nourishing herbs to my new mother friend to help with her healing.

I was able to show up BECAUSE of my shine. I was able to hold multiple crumblings for the women who matter most to me, all at once, because I was allowing myself to fully be in my shine.

Because when we shine, we are energised. We are inspired. And because of this, we are able to give to others.

This is why shining bright is such an important and underestimated act. It's so conditioned in women especially to play it down, to not take up space, to hide. And because of this, we are more likely to be defeated, depleted and lacking any real life-force energy to give to ourselves, let alone to anyone else.

But when we say yes to ourselves, YES to shining, we can create the ripples of change we desire in not only our own lives, but the lives of the women around us too.

And now, only a few months after my period of deep shine, I find myself sitting in that place of polarity. I am grieving my dog. I am moving through deep health challenges. I am moving through an intensely challenging period in my life. And now my beautiful friends are able to hold me, showing up for me the way I did for them. The outpouring of love we have received has been a force, and such a beautiful reflection of the people we have around us.

When I was moving through guilt around being in my shine while my loved ones were falling apart, not a single one of them questioned my brightness. Not for a second. They WANTED to celebrate me. They LOVED seeing me happy and sharing in my happiness with me. And they benefited from this because I was able to be there for them.

That said, this is a very new piece for me to sit in comfortably because in the past, I have felt anything but celebrated for my shine.

When I was pregnant and writing my first book, I was in a period of true shine. Life was life-ing in all of the best ways. I was deeply happy, so content, thriving in my health, my home life and my business. It was a true peak period of life for me, and I carried that energy with me everywhere I went.

During my pregnancy, I had four friends experience miscarriage at the same time. It was an awful piece to navigate and the guilt I felt each time was unimaginable. How cruel life was that I could be experiencing an easy and joyful pregnancy, and how unfair it was that my friends were grieving what I had. Polarity in motion.

It was my own doing when I decided that I didn't want to upset my friends any further, and so dodged pregnancy topics when they came up in conversation, or wore clothes that didn't cling to my stomach when I knew they would be around. I felt incredibly uncomfortable in my shine, so I downplayed it.

I know now that this was unnecessary. That my friends would have been able to hold my joy and their grief at the same time – this is life, after all. What I ended up experiencing from all but one friendship was a true, deep and solid appreciation for the joy in my life, while understanding and holding the grief in theirs.

That said, there was a friendship that never recovered from this experience. They were absolutely and understandably navigating their own challenges, while I was feeling immense guilt for enjoying a time in my life that should have been celebrated. I struggled, knowing my close friends and most family didn't even see me pregnant because of the lockdowns. I had no belly rubs from my favourite people, and my blessingway circle (a ceremonial circle of women dedicated to honouring a pregnant woman's transition from maiden to mother) was lacking at least eight of my dearest friends who were unable to travel at the time. We had no babymoon because we couldn't leave our home.

I needed to choose the shine I did have. This is such a vital component of shining brightly. We need to feel witnessed, celebrated and held in our shine. And we cannot expect to feel safe in doing that when worrying about people in our lives who cannot do that with us. I downplayed so much of my light, so much of my joy and brightness, for so many years, because over time I was so used to being belittled and diminished for the bright parts of me. The bright parts of me started to feel dangerous. I started to cringe at myself because of the cringing I was witnessing around me.

I had to choose: turn my light off, or end the friendship.

And I said yes to my light.

–

Before we look at what it takes to shine, and how to live in this way, it's important that we understand why we choose not to. Because while a life of true, bright, shiny magnetism might sound nice on the surface, for a lot of us, what it could mean to fully to step into it is why we avoid it.

If we were to take up space.

If we were to be seen – filters off, masks away – in the true, unedited versions of ourselves.

If we were to openly own the parts of ourselves that make us cringe.

Because – and we know this, but here's a reminder – we are conditioned to feel safe. And straying from the crowd does not feel safe. 'Fitting in' feels much safer. Belonging is paramount to our survival. And so we are intrinsically wired to play small, to not stand out from the crowd and to skirt around the edges of our true glow, because in our physical bodies (and likely our logical minds too), to stand out means to welcome attack.

And to be honest, this has happened to me more times than I can count.

I stepped back into modelling for the first time just after my thirtieth birthday. For context, my mother was a model (she was even crowned Miss Northern Beaches back in the 80s, get it, Mum!), and I was a child model growing up. I loved it. I love a camera, and walked my first Sydney Fashion Week catwalk when I was only seven (I was the youngest to walk that year). When I hit puberty, I started to get turned away from agencies as I developed a larger bust size, and – realistically, such was the industry at that time – because I didn't have blonde hair or blue eyes, and my body was curvy. The modelling dream was done for me, for more than 20 years, because I didn't fit in.

Then the industry started to make some long overdue (and still a long way to go) changes when it came to diverse representation. Suddenly, that dream of mine had legs again. I was so excited when I signed to management hitting 30 – an age where in the past, a model's career would be 'over' – yet mine was just kicking off. The nature of my body lends itself to booking swimwear and lingerie, which I love to do, and it was a time I was truly feeling in my shine.

That's when the trolling online started.

> 'You've always got your tits out, don't you have a husband?'
> 'Why are your eyebrows always raised like that, it's annoying – unfollowing!'
> 'One of your boobs looks like it's bigger than the other.'
> 'To be honest, I was thinking, "Who does she think she is?" when you said you were going to model …'

And these were the tame ones. At its worst, I received an anonymous email from a fake email address telling me that I was an embarrassment, and that this person and their friends found my Instagram stories hilarious because I clearly would do anything for attention. Someone else wrote anonymously on my website that my husband was cheating on me. People were literally out to get me, to make me feel shit. Taking the parts of me I was proudest of – the core of my shine – the beautiful love I had in my life, and my dream career aspirations coming to life, and shitting all over them.

Why?

Because I was shiny.

It was devastating. Here I was, in a period of my life that felt so shiny for me, and I was being publicly roasted. I would feel immense anxiety any time I went to upload a work photo – likely in a swimsuit, because that was my work at the time – knowing that, at the bare minimum, people would be talking about me behind my back. I was scared when a new comment would land on a post, or a new DM appeared in my inbox, because all of a sudden these actions felt threatening. What was this stranger online going to say about me? What judgement would I receive today?

But while the result of these comments were moments of tears and feeling small, I did it, despite it all. I did not shy away. I leaned in. I kept posting. I kept showing up. And not only because it was my job to – literally what I was getting paid to do – but because I knew that's what my system needed to really shine. That I'd be growing in my capacity to take up space and hold that space, no matter what was directed at me. Praise or criticism or otherwise. Taking up space for the sake of taking up space alone. Shining, despite it all. Expanding my window of tolerance. THAT'S the work.

Now, this was a conscious decision to show up, and I had the support around me to hold me through all I was processing as I navigated this part of my journey. I was seeing my kinesiologist regularly. I was practising EFT with Erin. I was leaning on all of the aforementioned practices in this book – meditation, journalling, daily body movement, the list goes on. So I had the foundation to hold myself through this tension. It's vital we do not confront these challenging parts of owning our light alone, especially if they feel anxiety-inducing. Working with a practitioner (or multiple practitioners) and friends and family that can hold you through this part of your journey is key.

As the law of polarity would have it, while I was on the receiving end of much criticism about my body, my career was skyrocketing. I was spotted on my first swim shoot by none other than Tash Oakley and Devin Brugman, who invited me to their Monday Swim Yacht party that week, one of the most coveted swimwear events in the modelling world (my agent was at a loss. How could one of their newest 'rookie' models nail an invite to an event that she couldn't even get for her best models?). I booked campaigns with some of my favourite brands. I was going to weekly castings and industry events and loving it. I was learning so much and holding my shine, despite the criticism. I kept showing up. I kept leaning in. And because of this, my capacity to hold my shine kept expanding. I wasn't contracting, so neither was life. It expanded alongside me. I felt shiny, and so life matched my shine.

It's only because of the deep work I had done to pre-empt this that I was able to hold the chaos of my inner shadows among the brightness I was stepping into.

I'm not exaggerating when I say I have sat in years of kinesiology sessions around this thread alone – around me shining. It is my greatest gift and my biggest struggle. To hold my brightness in the face of those who don't want to see it – and will publicly say so (in less kind terms). And I think it's so important to recognise this – that the shiny people in your life, be they friends or people you connect with online – are likely having to battle with themselves when it comes to conditioning around being 'too much', 'too loud', 'too sexy', 'too [*insert criticism here*]'. It's not that it isn't hard, but what we want out of our lives lies on the other side of the hard. The hard is the hurdle. And the path to get there is to jump over it and keep fucking going, every time it comes.

I first experienced mass public shaming when I was only 19. It was an age before Instagram or even Facebook, when YouTube was the main online platform. At the time, I had won a competition to be the 'It Girl' for a leading makeup brand and one of my videos for the brand ended up in pride of place on the YouTube Australia homepage. That is, if anyone in Australia logged on to YouTube at that time, the first thing they saw was my video. My face. My light.

When I was first made aware of this, I was so excited. What an opportunity! At the time, I was studying journalism and becoming a television presenter was top of my career list, so this felt aligned. On path. So right!

What started as a shiny moment, however, ended in tears in my bedroom late at night, scrolling through hundreds of awful comments about me and how I looked (and lots of nice ones, but we're not conditioned to remember those).

This happened 16 years ago and some of those comments still stick with me.

> 'She's UGLY!'
> 'She looks like a witch!'
> 'Why would anyone want her to be the face of their brand?'

And countless men commenting various sexual fantasies about what they would 'do to me' if they had the chance. It was horrific. I was a mess. The brand had to disable comments on the video because it was so bad.

And what that experience taught me – in my pure and innocent, naive and highly impressionable 19-year-old expression – was that being seen by the public wasn't safe. I'd be attacked for it. Strange men would want to do terrible things to me and women would hate me.

At this stage, I'd already spent my life being criticised and attacked for existing. Did I want to do that to myself again? Was it worth it?

Somewhere along the way, deep down I obviously told myself it wasn't. Over time, I stopped applying for the modelling agencies. I stopped going to the drop-in acting classes. I stopped looking for work experience in TV (even though my journalism university lecturer told me I was made to be a news anchor).

I gave it all up, even though those dreams live in my heart to this day. Because it didn't feel safe. Being seen – being myself – in a public way didn't feel safe. And we are wired to seek safety.

But, like we learned earlier in the book when discussing our window of tolerance when it comes to our nervous systems, the same rule applies here. The reality is that the way I wish to shine in my life *is* safe, for the most part. The parts of my life that desire bigness – the career aspirations, the thriving health, the abundant bank account, the beautiful family – are, in their essence, safe for me to hold. If we took conditioning away and just looked at the straight facts, I am safe for desiring these things, and I will be safe as they arrive for me.

The challenge doesn't actually lie in what being shiny specifically means to us, because we all hold varying ambitions, dreams and light, and so our personal definition of 'shining bright' will look different to each of us.

The challenge lies in what subconscious programs we have running in the background that are telling us that it's not safe to be bright. To stand out. To pursue our wildest dreams.

In working with thousands of women all over the world over the years, all desiring more for themselves, their families and their lives but feeling stifled by conditioning and subconscious limiting beliefs in some way or another, I can narrow it down to one of these common beliefs:

> *What will people (family, friends, strangers on the internet) think of me?*
> *I'll be judged/criticised for this.*
> *I don't want to be 'too much'.*
> *I don't feel like I am enough.*
> *I'm an imposter – who do I think I am to desire this/live this way?*
> *What if I fail?*

These are the root, subconscious beliefs most of us hold – either one, or perhaps all to some degree – when it comes to shining.

What will people think of me?

> *What if people think I'm weird?*
> *What if people don't like me?*
> *What if people think I'm full of myself?*
> *What if people are intimidated by me?*
> (These are all real-life examples submitted to me when I asked: *why are you afraid to shine?*)

What will people think of me? is one of the most common beliefs when it comes to taking up space, being seen and shining brightly in all of our weird and wonderful ways. I still face-off with a variation of this limiting belief almost daily. Every time I post something on my social media that shows my body in particular, because this has been the part of me that has received direct criticism and attack for my entire life. With that in mind, it's understandable to question what other people will think of us, especially if we have faced much criticism, or abuse. And to a degree, I don't believe this question around how we are perceived by others will ever disappear entirely. So long as we are human, we will care about what people think about us. It is literally embedded in our survival conditioning – to be safe is to belong. And so when we feel judged, criticised or attacked (even if that feeling is simply a perception), of course we do not feel safe. And so, more often than not, we will do the opposite of the thing that doesn't feel safe. In this case, we swap shining for shrinking. We hide.

I challenge the notion when people say, 'I don't care what people think of me.' I don't know that this is the end-goal here. To shine doesn't mean to shine in full acceptance of being disliked. God no. I feel sick at the thought of people not liking me. Despite that, I know I do things in my life that people *will* judge me for and that people won't like me for. The trick here is to show up in ways that expand my window of tolerance when it comes to my own self-imposed judgement.

At the time of writing this book, I am yet to announce to my social media community that I have signed with new modelling management. I have taken three years away from modelling while I navigated postpartum and new motherhood, and to step back into it at this stage in my life is equal parts shiny and terrifying. So I did a little experiment with myself, under the guidance of Britt. She challenged me to show up online in ways that would feel *cringe* in my system. Not because she wants me to feel like shit – quite the opposite, she wants the best for me and is genuinely one of my biggest cheerleaders. What Britt was challenging me to do here was to expand my window of tolerance in gentle ways, in order to train my brain to recognise what actually is safe to hold.

For me, this looked like starting to share more modelling content without any means of justifying why I was doing it. Headshots from a recent shoot. A beautiful black-and-white image of me in my bra. Styles of images I hadn't shared in years – and especially not since becoming a mother. Each time, I found myself coming up with excuses why I shouldn't. I needed to wait until my portfolio was ready, I needed people to know that this was my job now, I needed to explain how hard it was for me so people could see that, yes, I was shiny but I was also vulnerable …

But part of this exercise was to sit in the cringe. To not explain what I was feeling to anyone – under the guise of being understood or liked – but just to sit in it. To feel the discomfort. To feel at my edge. To watch the follower count drop (people always unfollow when I show up shiny, but we'll explore that later on). And to realise – despite all of those feelings moving through me – that I actually was fine. That in my cringe, it was okay. That in my light, I was safe.

I was sitting backstage at the play I was understudy for recently with one of the actors. He was feeling anxious because there were a group of people in the audience who he sensed would be judging him and his performance. When he shared this with me, do you know what I said to him? 'You're right. They probably *are* judging you.'

Because that's the truth of it. People are judging you. Not as much as they are judging themselves (I think we can all vouch for that, right?), but, to some degree, in some way, especially if you are stepping into shining in your life, you will be judged for it. Now maybe it won't be on a public platform like me. Maybe you'll just perceive the judgement (which is just as scary). Regardless, when you find yourself asking the question *what will people think of me?*, the truth of it is – they'll be thinking something. Good or bad. You'll likely never know.

So when it comes to this question, can you flip it instead? Can you ask yourself:

What do I think of me?

Now, depending on the level of deconditioning work you have done on this question, it will likely lead you to one of the following answers:

I'm too much – rooted in tall poppy syndrome

or

I'm not enough – rooted in imposter syndrome.

Let's look at these both, shall we?

Tall poppy syndrome

In a *Harper's Bazaar* article titled 'Breaking Down Tall Poppy Syndrome', tall poppy syndrome is described as a societal attitude that occurs when people are resented, disliked or criticised due to their successes.[38]

What's interesting to note about this term is that it is specifically an Australian and New Zealand term, which points intrinsically to cultural values we hold as a society around celebrating success, achievement and – overall – being bright and shiny.

38 harpersbazaar.com.au/tall-poppy-syndrome-wellbeing-mental-health

And this is why we, as Australians, feel it most. When I was first introduced to tall poppy syndrome, I was sitting in a kinesiology session around shining brightly specifically in modelling – more than seven years ago now. At this time, while I was aware that this phenomenon was absolutely playing out in my life, I was SO AFRAID to be seen in my brightness. What I wasn't aware of was the depth of the energetics of this concept, and why it is so rife in Australia specifically.

I believe the reason behind this lies in ley lines. Ley lines are energetic lines that geographically cross over one another across the globe, intersecting at sacred sites and holding undetectable, but prominent, sacred energies. Uluru and Kata Tjuta in the Northern Territory are two very culturally significant landmarks in this country, especially to the Aṉangu people, the Traditional Owners of the land. And when we look at the most prominent ley line in Australia, we are drawn right to them as well. This ley line specifically is known as the solar plexus ley line.[39]

This is where it gets interesting. The solar plexus chakra – for those of you unfamiliar with the seven energy centres that govern our body – is the yellow energy centre that sits in the centre of our stomach. Energetically, this centre represents our inner light. Our power. Our capacity to shine.

In my opinion, it is no coincidence that Australia has the highest energetic concentration of this chakra point in the world, and also has a collective of people struggling deeply with the wounding connected to this chakra: taking up space and stepping into our light. This isn't just an individual experience; it is a collective one too.

39 iamsahararose.com/blog/chakras-and-grids

And it's something we see constantly, especially with women and the LGBTQ community (really, anyone who isn't a white male, let's be real). That it's far too scary to be in our light because it's placing a target on our backs. We see it all the time in mass media, on Facebook threads, in forum comments. When Delta Goodrem was a judge on *The Voice* – beautiful, kind-hearted and incredibly talented – rather than being celebrated, she was constantly criticised in mass-rhetoric (maybe you even joined in?). She was annoying. She loved herself. I lost count of the amount of times I read, 'I just don't like her', without any reason.

I'll tell you why; it's because she was bright. It's because she was shiny. It's because she was beautiful (inside and out). It's because she was confident in herself. And when we see a woman in that energy – unapologetically so – in this country, we don't celebrate her. We tell her she's too much.

And this is where it all comes undone. Because the more we join in with this judgement and criticism of another's shine, the more we are diminishing our own light. The more we are witnessing someone being publicly disliked for 'being too much', the more we are building evidence for why being seen as being 'too much' is dangerous.

And the only way through it is to move to a different country where you're actually celebrated. I kid, I kid! It's actually much harder than that. It's to become okay with being 'too much'.

And how do we do that? Well, like anything we want to get better at – we practise it.

When I'm sharing a swimwear photo from a modelling shoot, or a poem I have written that people might not fully understand, or a life experience that is deeply vulnerable, I know that to some people, I will be perceived as 'too much'. In some moments I even perceive myself as being too much. I notice when these judgements arise. And I post anyway. I share anyway. I cringe through the too-muchness, knowing that my light lies on the other side of it. And knowing that it is my responsibility to actively choose my light, every time.

People will fall away. I am far more likely to grow my community online when I am sharing my darkness, the shadows I have traversed, the vulnerability. Misery likes company, or so the saying goes. And that is okay. I will always share my challenges, my shadow, my vulnerabilities – I think that's quite apparent reading this book. I don't shy from the shadow. On the flip side, I also refuse to shy from the light. I am well aware that when I share something that feels shiny to me, it could come across as too bright to others. And they won't want to see that. So I let people come and go. I share for me. I share to build my own capacity to hold my light, and my dark – my full-spectrum polarity.

I don't know that tall poppy syndrome is actually going anywhere. So unfortunately, when it comes to this as one of our greatest challenges to taking up space and being seen in our light, waiting for the time we don't feel beholden to it is just not going to happen.

It's about showing up *despite* the cringe. Despite the fear. Despite the judgement. Expanding your own capacity to hold that and not shrinking when it comes (in whatever form it takes). Because the judgement will come, one way or another. So using your fear of that isn't a valid excuse. How can you hold that fear – move through that fear – rather than wait on the sidelines of your life for it to miraculously no longer exist?

The opposite of tall poppy syndrome? Celebration. Taking up big, bright and shiny unapologetic space. It's so important we put ourselves in energies and environments that mirror to us that it's safe to be celebrated, it's safe to shine in the way we are desiring to. Therein lies the building of our own permission to shine (thank you, Bachelor Girl, for the anthem we all need).

I have two vision boards in front of me. One is a standard board that captures all of my biggest dreams right now. The other is entirely dedicated to images of models who feel bright and shiny to me, because this is the specific area of my life right now I need to feel safe to shine in. I am following women like Ashley Graham and engaging with content by Florence Given because these are the bright and shiny women I use as anchors when I am wanting to step more into my own bright and shininess.

In that same *Harper's Bazaar* article, Dr Rumeet Billan, author of 2018 study 'The Tallest Poppy', is quoted as saying, 'Where people experienced TPS the most was with their friends and social network, which raises the question as to who we choose to keep as our friends and why. What ends up happening for some is they stop sharing their milestones with those whom they should feel comfortable confiding in due to a fear of being resented, attacked or ostracised.'[40]

For me, I no longer entertain friendships that cannot celebrate me in all of my shine. If I am finding myself cutting my poppy down (so to speak) in the company of anyone, I instantly know they are not for me. When it comes to feeling safe to shine, community is everything. It's no longer good enough to be

40 harpersbazaar.com.au/tall-poppy-syndrome-wellbeing-mental-health

wearing diluted masks with some people in our lives because they cannot handle the brightness.

I *know* of people in my own life who are still screenshotting posts of women doing amazing, shiny things online and sending them around to their friends, making fun of them. I have likely been screenshotted and made fun of, let's be real. It's our responsibility to do better. Call it out. Don't engage in tall poppy syndrome rhetoric. CELEBRATE one another. If there is a woman online who you feel *cringed* by (my new word), ask yourself why. Is it because she is taking up space that feels stretchy for you? It's not good enough to say, 'I just don't like her' or 'She's annoying'. Ask yourself why. And the answer here likely lies in the parts of you that you are diminishing.

We are the company we keep. The antidote to this syndrome is to look directly at your community – your friends, your family, your online networks. Who celebrates you? Who do you feel unsafe to share your wins with? And perhaps it's time to make some adjustments.

Maybe it's time for a new community.

–

I was 18 months postpartum when I found myself scrolling social media on the hunt for local drama classes. I hadn't stepped foot in an acting class in more than 15 years, and yet somehow the emptiness I felt in postpartum had lead me back to seeking pieces of me I once clung to for joy and light. I didn't feel like myself anymore, because I wasn't who I used to be. I had been through the most intense initiation of my life – I was still unravelling it, in fact – and yet, at this stage I started desiring 'more'. I was seeking joy. Something that was 'mine', outside of being the mother or the business owner. Something that got me out of the house, that had me around people and energy that felt inspiring and fun and new, and something that I had been yearning for, for years and years and years.

I was stopped in my tracks when I found an advertisement for a local theatre company sharing that they were taking applications for auditions for their next play. I clicked in and out of that page countless times before holding my breath, filling out the application, and hitting 'send'. It felt stretchy of me to even consider auditioning for something when I hadn't been on stage since my Year 12 musical (I was Marty in *Grease*, thank you very much). I didn't know of anyone up here who was part of the theatre company. And I had very little experience and was a new mother who had lost all idea of who she was. Surely I wouldn't get an audition.

When the email landed in my inbox inviting me to audition that weekend, I felt equal parts ecstatic and sick to my stomach. The morning of the audition was one of the most intense anxiety spirals I'd had in years. What was I doing? Should I just not go? The audition process was over a half-day and would involve script work (love) and improvisation (I die, I die, I die!). What the HELL was I doing?!

I sent off panicked texts of nerves to a few of my friends, who all replied encouraging me and celebrating me for saying yes to something my heart was so clearly desiring (for so many years), even among the intensity of the fear and the nerves. The entire drive to the audition, I was beside myself. I kept telling myself I was just showing up to push through the fear – to show myself that my joy was important, and despite how edgy this felt, I was safe. It was an exercise in my capacity to hold something that felt equal parts terrifying and exciting.

I walked into that hall not knowing a single person. I was dying on the inside as it was obvious I was one of only a few who didn't know anyone. Everyone was clearly friends, hugging and chatting and catching up and squealing when someone else entered the audition room. I awkwardly walked over to a bench and sat beside someone who introduced herself as Bonnie. She was lovely and chatty and bubbly and also didn't know anyone, but unlike me, she was exuding confidence and wasn't scared of improv at all (I later learned that she was an improv actor, so fair enough).

Those four hours flew by. I spent them in pure joy – total play, flow and connection. I drove home with the biggest smile on my face. I wasn't even thinking about getting a part – I'd pushed myself outside of my comfort zone and done something just for me. That activated my shine in ways I hadn't yet experienced in postpartum, and that was more than I could have asked for. What lay on the other side of my trepidation was my light returning to me. What a gift that was.

When I received the email offering me a role in the play, I cried. Finally – finally – I felt a semblance of myself returning in ways I hadn't ever realised I was longing for. The production went on to win multiple awards for best local theatre production, and one of my scenes was nominated for best moment in theatre. When the show ended, I walked away with new friends – a community of creative people I could be my whole self with. A community of people who also had big dreams, and who wanted to see one another shine. I finally understood what community felt like. And it just got better from there.

The next time auditions rolled around, I was no longer terrified. I was nervous, for sure, but now it was me walking into the audition room squealing and hugging all of my (new) friends. When I was offered the role of understudy for all four lead female roles, I didn't hesitate in accepting it. I was keen for whatever involvement I could have – if that meant wearing blacks and running props on between scenes, then I was all in (and this is what I did, too!). And while I never took to the stage on this production, that wasn't the point. Because I was walking away with connection and creative community. People who got me. People who are committed to their own shine, and in celebration of one another's.

Only last night, I was out with two of my beautiful friends from the company, chatting well into the night about anything and everything – our creative visions, projects we want to work on together, our involvement in the next production, how excited we are to be united as a 'family' once more. Bonnie, from that very first audition, is one of my dear friends, visiting me weekly for cacao and chats, keeping me company while I'm stay-at-home mumming.

And this is the gift of creative community. What lies on the other side of it is the biggest permission slip to shine. The greatest permission slip to be bright. And the celebration of creating something together, as a team. This energy becomes contagious. We want more of it. It spurs us on in all of the best ways – to seek more opportunities to shine, to be bright, to celebrate one another. It's why 'come downs' after any production are such a real thing. Because the energetic high you experience while you're in a creative community bubble is some of the greatest, most uplifting energy you can feel. And that's because we're all allowing ourselves to be big, to be bright, to shine.

I have friends in my life now who have witnessed the transformation in me following my foray into local theatre and have felt inspired to pick up their own creative projects and establish their own creative communities. One is taking DJ lessons (in her 40s, no less!), another is taking dance classes for the very first time in her life (in her 30s). Another went along to an improv class. I am of such a deep belief now that to fully shine – to fully show up in our brightness – a component of creative outlet (with a side of community) is not just a nicety. It's a necessity. We must harness spaces where we feel entirely safe to be all of ourselves – in pure play, joy and creative flow. This is what harmonises any trepidation we have about being ourselves. Finding spaces where all of us is not only welcome, but celebrated.

I didn't realise it at the time, but in joining the local theatre company in new motherhood, I started to shape my life around a concept known as identity diversity. Identity diversity refers to an individual diversifying their sense of self, interests and values across a range of means and interest areas. This allows for the individual to have a more varied sense of self, and be less inclined to have a total identity breakdown, should all of their eggs crack in their one basket (my shift into motherhood, for example).

Brad Stulberg, author of *Master of Change: How to Excel When Everything Is Changing, Including You*, explains: 'The more you define yourself by any one activity the more fragile you become. If that activity doesn't go well – or when there is inevitable chaos or change – you lose a sense of who you are. The opposite is "self-complexity", a term researchers use for having multiple components to your identity. The key to a strong identity is to diversify your sense of self.'[41]

41 thegrowtheq.com/rugged-flexibility-and-diversifying-your-sense-of-identity

Tim Ferriss is another thought leader who speaks to this concept, explaining that it's 'smart to diversify your identity, to invest your self-esteem and what you care about into a variety of different areas – business, social life, relationships, philanthropy, athletics – so that when one goes south, you're not completely screwed over and emotionally wrecked'.[42]

These days, identity diversification is at the forefront of my life. No longer are my eggs in one basket when it comes to how I define myself. I have my local theatre outlet and the beautiful community that comes with that. I also happen to be co-producing the next musical production, which is an actual childhood dream come true I would have never realised if I hadn't gone along to that very first audition.

I have my family unit, and the true joy I feel now as a stay-at-home mother. When I am in mum mode, my business does not exist. I am hyper available to my little girl when I wear that hat, and can fully surrender to that time and space, knowing I have other outlets for me outside of mothering, so I am not 'just' a mother.

I have my cooking, another hobby I picked up off the back of writing my last book and realising my hobbies were minimal. I cook with my husband, with my little girl and on my own. It brings me such joy and is such an important part of my life. It is a practice that connects me to my Maltese heritage and memories I have of my nanna in her kitchen. It is a hobby and a creative outlet that is just for me.

I have my spiritual community, the women I have connected with (online and off) when I was a practising psychic. We drink cacao together, we pull cards together, we sit in ritual together,

42 markmanson.net/why-you-should-care-about-many-things

and we talk about wild esoteric practices together. We clear one another's energy fields and swim naked under waterfalls (well, not really, but it's on the list!). My soul feels deeply fulfilled and witnessed when exploring this side of me.

I have my modelling outlet, another creative means of expression that is also a work form for me, and allows me to indulge in my love of beauty, clothing and storytelling. I have friends I have made through modelling alone, who I would have never met otherwise, and we connect in very different ways to the ways I connect with my spiritual friends, or my mothering friends, for instance.

And I have my business world. The one world that I defined myself by before motherhood. And the one that came crashing down around me when motherhood beckoned. My business life takes up less space than ever, and that feels good for me. I can barely believe I am writing this, as only two years ago, feeling it crumble all around me was one of the darkest moments of my life. Everything I had defined myself by – my ability to make six figures, my ability to sell out online programs, my ability to provide for myself and my partner, my ability to help people all over the world, my ability to create and create and create and sell and sell and sell – all fell away. And I know now that it had to, because I was doing myself a disservice by only seeing my own innate value in how much money I could make, and how successful that made me as a businesswoman, and therefore as a person.

I am so much more than that. And so are you – be it business, motherhood or a relationship you define yourself by. It doesn't matter. Because you are so much more than that. You are all of the sum parts of your life story in equal, shiny measure. You are all of your passions and curiosities and creative outlets and backstories, regardless of whether it makes you money or not.

Your soul purpose is not purely to make money and that be it. Your soul purpose is not to raise your children and that be it. Your soul purpose is to cultivate a life of love. And we find that, through shining, through exploring all of the parts of ourselves that desire light – not just one part.

This is why I get so worked up when I read what I believe to be damaging rhetoric online, aimed at mothers in particular, around 'surrendering to the season you're in' when it comes to motherhood. Because while well-intended I'm sure, what this claim does is set mothers up for a complete identity crumble when their children grow up. You have likely seen this in your own life, with mothers who have gone before you. When we lay all of our eggs in the basket of motherhood, we are forgetting the parts of ourselves that are not only a mother. The parts that are a creative. The parts that are a lover. The parts that are passionate and smart and inspired. And yes, you can find all of these things in motherhood, but if this is the only space in your life you are finding them (because 'it's just a season'), then we are completely ignoring the proven psychological impacts of not having and maintaining identity diversity. This is why divorce rates are so high in both new parenthood and after the kids leave home. This is why mothers experiencing menopause around the same time as their children flying the nest feel so incredibly depressed and empty, without purpose. Because piling all of your eggs into the basket of mother is a recipe for identity crisis down the track.

Motherhood is not 'just a season'. It is the rest of our lives. And to truly shine within that, we must find creative outlets, communities and pieces of the life puzzle that feel meaningful and give us depth and richness of a full-spectrum life experience, so that we do not crumble when our children leave home.

(Not to mention that this is an exceptionally privileged statement to make. For those of us who have to continue working, those of us who live in less-than-ideal living environments, those of us with inflamed thyroids and decades of trauma to unpack, surrendering to the season can actually be the worst thing to possibly do. We need to diversify. We need creative communities, businesses, side projects, hobbies and friendships that are just ours, and may have absolutely nothing to do with the fact we are also a mother.)

We are the company we keep, yes. And we are also the creative outlets we have, and the communities we are part of. We are multifaceted beings. And embracing this, rather than stifling it, is our key to shining.

Imposter syndrome

The dictionary defines imposter syndrome as 'the persistent inability to believe that one's success is deserved or has been legitimately achieved as a result of one's own efforts or skills.'[43] The term was first used in the 1970s by psychologists Suzanne Imes and Pauline Rose Clance, and today is one of the key reasons used when people explain why they aren't pursuing the life they desire. Why they are choosing to not shine, not dream big, not do the thing their heart desires. Maybe you've even used it yourself?

43 pmc.ncbi.nlm.nih.gov/articles/PMC8922383

But is the feeling of being an imposter, a fraud, a fake or phoney actually the piece here? Because chances are, we ALL feel like we are winging it, to some degree. Life is one big 'winging it', in my opinion. We try the thing, we're shit at the thing, we get better at the thing, we nail the thing. At least, that's my life equation for success (thank me later).

Or does something lie beneath the surface excuse of 'I have imposter syndrome'?

We never want to use labels like these as a cop-out as to why we aren't doing something that, deep down, we really want to do. It isn't enough to slap on the label of 'imposter syndrome' like a bumper sticker, and that be that. We need to dive deeper.

And it starts – as it often does – with getting curious. Asking why. Why do you feel like an imposter?

Rooted in *who am I to be brilliant?* and *what makes me special?*, imposter syndrome is deeply entrenched in the belief of not being enough, and not feeling worthy.

Likely somewhere along the way, you will start to identify one of the following limiting beliefs that are running the show:

> *I'm a high achiever and this feels new and uncomfortable for me.*
> *I'm used to excelling and I'm not sure I will excel at this.*
> *I don't feel 'good enough' (replace with 'worthy enough', 'smart enough', 'funny enough' etc.).*

Or, likely the undercurrent of all of these pieces:

> *What if I fail?*

I took to my Instagram stories to ask my online community (hi, guys!) what their main reasons for holding back from shining were. And while the large majority I had already recognised myself, one took me by immense surprise. And it was this: *what if I fail?*

I was so incredibly taken aback by the volume of women holding this belief closely – that to pursue the big, shiny life means they might fail, and that is far too scary to consider – that I forgot that this was a large part of my life too. I forgot what it was like to fear failure – because I don't anymore. I'm great at failing. But it hasn't always been this way.

The first and only time I failed a test was in high school. It was a maths test, typically, and I was in Year 11. I was so upset that I had a panic attack and had to sit in the year coordinator's office to calm down (shout out, Ms Wakeling!). I was devastated. I felt like my entire world was crumbling in on me. I was a failure. And I had spent my entire life forming an identity around not being a failure. I was the good girl, yes, and I was also the high achiever. Top of the class. I was the girl on stage at the end of year awards day walking away with countless trophies – and I'd been that way since I won my very first English competition when I was ten – getting 100 per cent and being part of only two per cent of the state to achieve such an outcome. I was celebrated so much, we ended up getting a puppy because my parents were so proud. Life felt in harmony and so, with that experience, I learned that to deal with the tumultuous energy of my life and bring it into balance, all I had to do was achieve, achieve, achieve.

And so set the wheels in motion for a lifetime of achievement. This didn't come without hard work – not at all. I skipped most of my adolescence in favour of studying. I slept with my notes under my pillow, practised essay writing and was highly competitive with my peers. If I didn't feel like my home life was thriving, I could feel like my academic life was. I was achieving and so I felt good enough. But also – even deeper than that – it felt safe when I could bring an achievement home to my family. Because that meant I'd be celebrated, and that meant I belonged, and perhaps the tension would ease, even for just a moment.

So my panic attack when I failed my maths test wasn't because I failed my maths test. It's because of what I'd made it mean about me. It meant no longer was I enough (even though, of course I was). It meant I didn't belong. It meant I was unsafe.

I didn't get good at failing until I left my corporate career and pursued running my own business. Because when running your own business, to do it well, you have absolutely no choice but to sit in the feelings of being an imposter, and lean into the likelihood of failure.

I had a Bachelor's Degree in Communications majoring in Writing under my belt, as well as five years of corporate experience and two years of work experience at leading magazines when I found myself back in retail working behind the counter of a jewellery store. At the time, I knew something had to change in my work life, and honestly a dip into retail felt like a huge exhale on my nervous system. But I did experience an ego death. My ego came crumbling down those first few shifts, any time I stood behind the counter of my local shopping centre, watching my peers from school walk past. I wanted to scream at them that this job wasn't forever, that I had just been made redundant and I was really physically unwell …

It was like I needed to justify my current life choices when, honestly, I'm now certain no one cared. But I cared. Well, at least my ego did.

This is what lies beneath imposter syndrome: the ego's desperate clinging to what feels safe and known (in my case, high achievement). Our ego's desperate clinging to external validation. Our ego's desperate clinging to a semblance of belonging.

What I hadn't known at that time was this ego death was making me a better person. A less judgemental, ego-centric version of me was being born. A version of me that didn't judge other people for what they did for work, or how much money they made.

Since this first ego-crumbling, I have experienced failure upon failure upon failure. I walk straight on into the flames of getting it wrong and I don't fear it. Because at this stage in my life, I can't afford to let a fear of failure be the thing that stops me from pursuing my greatest desires. Failure is the only way forward. If you aren't failing, you aren't trying – and if you aren't trying, then things will never change.

And I know if you are reading this book, this is not what you desire. You desire change. You desire your light back on. You desire to be bright and shiny and have your beautiful, bold, big dreams fulfilled. You want to choose you.

Well, guess what? The only way to experience these things is to become friends with failure. That's right; the only way to shine your brightest light in the world is to try things out, get things wrong and keep going despite it all. It's about not making it mean anything other than how courageous we are to give things a go. I will say it again: the light, the success and the brightness you desire in your life lies on the other side of failure. You need to become okay with getting it wrong. And the only way we can do that is to show ourselves it's okay to get it wrong.

I was first approached to put a book proposal together six years ago. At the time, my ego was so tied up in becoming a 'published author' that I didn't even stop to think if I had anything worth writing about. A publisher wanted to meet with me! This was a dream come true! Following this meeting, I put a clunky, clumsy proposal together with no real solid concept for a book, not thinking of anything other than 'I'm going to be an author!'

So you can imagine the ego-death that followed when I received an email from the publisher saying they had presented my concept to the sales team, and it was rejected. I was devastated. I was a failure. And my ego? Well, she was experiencing another crumble.

What followed that experience was two years of me going out and living my life. Writing for the joy and the love of it. Sharing words on my social media just because. I realised I didn't need the title of 'author' to be a writer – that was what I loved to do after all, and so I wrote. Not for money. Not for accolades. For me.

It's no surprise that two years after that first rejection, the same publisher (who is still my publisher today, shout out, Kel!) came back and asked me for another book proposal. This time I had a solid concept. And I was also seriously non-attached to becoming an author. I was six weeks pregnant and very sick and couldn't comprehend writing a book while I was growing a child. And yet this is what happened. My ego was out of the picture, and my dream landed in its place.

The necessary ego-crumbling of that very first rejection made me a better writer, a better author, gave me inspired content for my first book and also – dare I say it – made me a better person.

You could perceive my initiation into motherhood as one big failure. Where I intended to have a natural, zero-intervention, calm homebirth (and let me tell you, I did ALL of the 'work' to support this outcome), I ended up in a hospital transfer, obstetrician-supported, epidural-in-my-back-legs-in-stirrups-forceps-pulling-my-baby-out birth. Where I planned to breastfeed exclusively, and had not even considered the potential of needing to bottle – let alone formula – feed, I ended up having to rely on other women's breastmilk and formula to literally keep my child alive. Where I gathered I would dive straight back into work after three months of postpartum rest, I ended up throwing creation upon creation to the wall, with nothing sticking, no sign-ups and no money being made. Just when I thought my ego couldn't die any more, another mass crumbling would take the previous crumbling's place.

My motherhood initiation could be perceived as one giant failure – if you were to compare it to what I desired. But three years after the fact, and I don't see it as failure at all. I see each of these moments as another opportunity for my ego to die, and my light to grow. I see the courage it took for me to face life in these moments, and show up despite the pain, the identity dissolution, the embarrassment of things not working out for me, like they seemed to effortlessly work out for the people around me. Each of these crumblings has made me a stronger, more compassionate version of myself – to myself, and everyone around me. And to take it further, it is these experiences that have shaped this second book. Without them, who knows where I would be? But I know that because of them – because of the darkness I moved through – I am able to now experience and hold far more light than I ever have before. I am a better mother, a better friend, a better writer and a better person for them.

In any moment where I catch myself shrinking because of fear (of judgement – that's my big one, at least), I remind myself what I've been through to get here. What I would have given in those dark moments to shine again. I remind myself that I owe it to all parts of me – especially the parts of me that traversed such rough terrain – to be my brightest self.

Because life won't ever be a constant stream of bright, just as it won't be continuously dark. Like the breath, the seasons, the moon, or any being of a cyclic nature – we ebb and we flow. We inhale and we exhale. We fail and we succeed. We are light and we are shade. This is the law of shining brightly. To become okay with the opposite of that, knowing that this is life, and that both are equally as important for a full-spectrum, human experience.

Become okay with failing and you will become okay with shining.

–

Now that we've identified the key reasons why we're holding ourselves back from shining, let's dive into what MAKES us shine.

I hear you. *How, Hollie? How do I cultivate confidence? How do I emulate authentic expression? How do I share freely? How do I pursue my greatest, deepest, boldest desires?*

I took to my online community and asked them: *what is it that makes a person shiny in your life?* The answers are far less complex than you may think.

- Their energy (glowing, positive, uplifting, warm) and how it makes me feel
- Their genuine smile
- Their kindness
- When they're happy for my happiness, and never hide their own (happiness)
- They're like sunshine
- When someone talks about something they are passionate about
- Bright, fun people
- Engaging – they listen
- They are inhabiting more of themselves than most other people
- They know their worth
- They're confident and comfortable in their own skin
- They're vulnerable and authentic
- They embody their truth
- They believe anything is possible
- They aren't afraid to dream.

We are so great at overcomplicating things when, in reality, the answer is simple. When you think of the shiniest people in your life, what do they have in common?

How their energy makes you feel. Their kindness. Their inner beauty. Their soul.

The shiniest people aren't necessarily the prettiest or the richest or most intelligent. The shiniest people aren't the 'best' at everything, they aren't perfect, and heck – they all make mistakes, and likely also share these, openly and vulnerably. They celebrate you because they are happy for you, and they know your own shine won't take away from theirs.

The shiniest people are the people who show up and embody the truth of who they are, in its full spectrum. In an era of artificial intelligence, they are the antithesis of embodied *authentic expression*. And not authenticity as the overused buzzword – if you're genuinely showing up as your authentic self, you don't need to describe yourself as authentic. People can feel when someone is being real. People can sense when someone is being honest. People love to feel genuine connection with someone, when they know they are being met with genuine expression.

To shine isn't to do anything more than embrace – and express – all of you.

It's holding eye contact with someone when you are in conversation, and genuinely listening curiously to what they have to say.

It's smiling at the waitress as she serves you your breakfast and waving goodbye to the person you had small talk with at the bus stop.

It's saying, 'I'm not doing great,' when someone asks you how you're feeling, and you're having a really hard time.

It's not apologising for your tears when they fall in public.

It's wearing an outfit you feel beautiful in, no matter the 'occasion', because you realise that to live is the occasion.

It's practising patience – not just with others, but mostly with yourself – in the moments you are not shiny, and at the times you get it wrong. Because hey, you tried. And that takes courage.

It's listening to your favourite music and dancing in the car at the traffic lights, even though the people in the car beside you are staring.

It's being okay to go first. To look the fool. To get it wrong. And to do it all anyway.

The shiniest people shine not because they're actively trying to, but because they have chosen to live their lives as unapologetically as possible. And because of this, they have cultivated an energy that is genuine. In this genuine energy, they have also cultivated warmth. Their shine is not just a means of expression for themselves but a permission for every other person they touch, to also shine in their own lives.

Between writing stints at my favourite cafe, I took a little break to wander through the local markets. I was greeted at the gate by a familiar face – we call him the 'banana man' – a local who, without fail, shows up to every community event wearing his tie-dye shirt, shaking his banana maracas and singing, 'have a beautiful day at the markets today' on loop – all while hula hooping, no less. His energy is contagious. I challenge anyone to pass him and not crack a smile (or, if you're also unapologetic, have a dance with him!). Everyone up here knows him – because of his energy. It is unapologetic. It is warm. It puts a smile on the faces of everyone who passes him. He shines. And he shares his shine with the world in a way that is (very) uniquely his.

You know what I find most fascinating about this? I don't even know his name. I don't follow him on social media (I'm not sure he even has it?). I'm not up to date with his day-to-day life happenings. But I know him because of his energy. Because of the way he is choosing to show up and share his light in the world. Because I have personally been impacted by his light many, many times.

I can say the exact opposite for many people I have come in contact with (this is absolutely not all of them, but there are more than you would think) who have some semblance of public persona or image – call them influencers or famous people, whatever you choose – who have the big online platforms, the perceived 'success', the highlights reels – and who, behind the scenes, do not emit a true, honest shine. Sure, the filters and the paparazzi photos (that are often staged, just a heads-up) can elevate someone's persona to a degree, and have people assume that they are 'shiny' because of their popularity, but what I'm coming to realise is shininess – true, real, embodied shininess – has absolutely nothing to do with how well-known you are online. It has nothing to do with how many followers you have, how often you post on your social media, how many times someone recognises you in the street.

Shininess has everything to do with who you are when there isn't a camera to capture it. Shininess is humble. It isn't forced. You can't filter shine, because it moves from the inside, out. To shine is all about intention. And more often than not, the shiniest people are living their true, aligned values with positive intention at the forefront. They want to leave the world better than they found it. They want to be present with the people they love. They want to give back to their communities. They aren't the type to virtue signal or to jump on the latest trend because that's what will get them more engagement on their reels. They are the ones consistently paving their *own* paths, their *own* passions, their *own* trends and their *own* causes. In a world that is begging for real among a sea of dishonest, the shiny people are continuing to live their lives the way they always have. With their truth at the forefront. In spite of what anyone else's truth may be.

This is where it is important that we start to identify where we have placed someone else on a pedestal of 'better than' ourselves. Because we are ALL valid and deserving of a life we truly desire. We are ALL capable of living beyond our wildest dreams. And when we catch ourselves naysaying, demanding, 'Who am I to shine?' – I want you to remember: who are you NOT to?

When we pedestal another person (be it public figure, celebrity, mentor, or anyone else in our life we admire), we are willingly handing over our own power – our own light – to that person. We are saying to ourselves, 'They are deserving, but I am not.' Years ago now, when pedestalling still ran rife in my life, a public figure in the personal development space I really admired started DMing me. SHE wanted to chat to ME? She wanted to be my friend?! I remember being on the phone to my coach at the time, proclaiming, 'I just don't get it. She's amazing. Why would she want anything to do with me?'

In that outward expression of such a deep-seated belief, what was actually playing out was feeling unworthy of shining. Of brightness. Of wronging myself for desiring to be big and seen. All traits I saw in this person, but I didn't see in me. And a diluting of my own power, brilliance and shine because I didn't feel good enough – especially in comparison to the people I was pedestalling.

The pedestalling often is our key to identifying what you desire in another person – perhaps witnessing the reasons we admire them, absolutely. But then – rather than feeling that because they emulate these pieces, it makes them 'better than' we are – how can we start to question how we also have these traits within us?

I have this story that has played out my entire life that I am not the 'cool girl'. I can be the smart girl, absolutely. The kind girl, yes. The funny girl – obviously. But the cool girl? God no. I've never connected with that sentiment because I have never felt 'cool'. And so, any time anyone I have pedestalled as 'cool' shows me a semblance of recognition or connection, I get suss. I become awkward, I freeze. I feel uncomfortable. Because the pedestalling of this person completely wipes out my capacity to hold my own (kind of uncool) light. That maybe I'm not 'cool' in the way I define it myself – having the latest, trendy fashion pieces, being invited to coveted events, embodying a level of confidence I am yet to reach.

But that is what makes me different. Not less than. Unique. Not below.

I don't have to be the 'cool girl' in the way I have defined it. And I can still embody my shine despite considering myself as uncool, or others as 'more cool' than me.

Do you see the difference? Maybe for you, it isn't the cool people you pedestal. Maybe it's the smart people. The 'successful' people. The people who are living a life you desire but aren't quite there yet. Can you recognise this in them, and still recognise that you are also worthy of all of these things, despite not being there yet? That these people you are pedestalling are not actually 'better than' you – but just embodying a certain characteristic, trait or lifestyle that you are desiring? Can you let yourself desire that, despite not having it yet?

Let's break down all of the ways we can say yes to our own shine, in the context of what it actually means to be shiny.

To emit warm energy

Well, we have already been through an entire chapter on this exact intention. Our energy is our personal 'business card' and how we make people feel when they are in our energetic frequency is a direct mirror of how we practise cultivating solid energetic hygiene (and how well we know ourselves and what our energy needs in any given moment). Our energy is supposed to be uniquely ours – not diluted by others, and not mimicking someone else's energy we like, admire or pedestal. Our energy is ours. Getting to understand what makes it unique (through modalities like astrology and human design), and what both fuels us and depletes us, is key to cultivating an energetic resonance that is both warm, and memorable. Our energy is EVERYTHING. Including how we make others feel. Including our capacity to shine.

I love this insight that landed by my good friend and incredible astrologer Jules Ferrari when I asked, 'What makes someone shiny?'

She shared: *They are inhabiting more of themselves than most other people.*

When I asked her to explain, she said:

> One way we could think of this is that as beings, we have our own unique operating software. Part of what is vital to learn is how do you run your own energy? How do you process and regenerate your energy? What makes you feel most alive?
>
> In a society that really encourages us to live from the outside first, to take in the information of the world and adapt to it, it is a very attractive quality to be centred within yourself, conscious and aware, living from the inside – out. In astrology, our Sun is a symbol of consciousness. If you have brought that spotlight of consciousness into the layers of your own self, there is more space for you to shine from. Part of 'doing the work' and 'being conscious' is making friends with your individual operating software.

Let it be that simple. Become more of who you are. Get to know yourself from the inside, out rather than the other way around. Spend time contemplating the inner workings of your world – what makes you, you. And lean on modalities that illuminate the depths, nuance and truth of who you are (like astrology and human design) to deepen your relationship with your true energy.

When you embody that, and choose to live with that at the forefront, your warmth shines without effort. Because you are embodied in truth.

To practise kindness

The thing about kindness is firstly, not to mistake it for niceness. Let's look at the difference between the two.

> **kindness**[44] / noun
> the quality of being friendly, generous, and considerate
>
> **niceness**[45] / noun
> the quality of being nice; pleasantness

I have found in my line of work – especially having written a book on people-pleasing – that niceness is often the piece people pleasers will land on when we put a smile on our face and 'do the right thing', whether we actually want to do it or not. We fall back on being the 'nice girl' as a mask which hinders our capacity to be truthful and honest about our feelings. We can lean on being the 'nice one' to a fault, and oftentimes this niceness can dilute the full spectrum of our human experience.

44 en.bab.la/dictionary/english/kindness
45 www.vocabulary.com/dictionary/niceness

Kindness enables us to lean on the qualities of friendliness, consideration and generosity, when we have the capacity to do so. You can be kind and hold really strong, solid boundaries that you don't override to appear 'nice'. You can kindly say no to commitments you don't want to attend. Kindness lives in our honesty, with ourselves and with those around us. Kindness isn't something that can be forced – it is embodied.

Some questions to consider here:

Are you kind to yourself?

What are the words you use when you speak to yourself or about yourself? Only last week I caught myself jokingly proclaiming how much of an idiot I was, but to the point where I counted four times in a single day where I had said – aloud – 'I'm such an idiot.' I had to stop myself in my tracks and call myself out on it, because it is far from kind. I wouldn't ever speak to my little girl this way, so why was I speaking to myself like this?

I reminded myself that I actually wasn't an idiot at all, and apologised to myself as if I were talking to my daughter. We are the words we speak (but you know that from my first book, don't you?). Make them kind.

Are you kind to your loved ones?

When you are connecting with your loved ones, are you practising full presence or are you half-in, half-out? On a social dinner out, do you leave your phone in your bag on Do Not Disturb, or is it face down next to your plate?

When someone is in conversation with you, are you waiting for your turn to speak, or are you genuinely listening and offering them support as a sounding board? Do you celebrate their successes? Their birthdays? Do you remember to check in on the big moments they are navigating? Do you show up when you say you will? Do you compliment them? Do you send flowers because they're going through a hard time – or even 'just because I love you'.

There is so much to be said about loving on our loved ones even more – especially in an age where we are feeling more disconnected than ever before. Can you make it a commitment to your relationships to practise kindness more?

Are you kind to strangers?

When was the last time you offered kindness to a stranger, without expecting anything in return? Random acts of kindness have been proven to elevate feelings of happiness – and there are so many easy ways to do this. Smile at a stranger on your next walk, without expecting them to offer one in return (throw in a cheeky hi if you're feeling stretchy!). Pay for the person's coffee in line behind you (I've even paid for someone's tank of petrol before!). Buy the beaded bracelet from the little girl's street-side stall even though it won't fit you. Make a commitment to donate to, or volunteer regularly for, a charity of your choice (my business supports a local animal sanctuary).

The thing about kindness is, it's not something that you need to proclaim you do – no one in my life excluding my husband knows these acts I've shared (well, now all of you do too!) – because kindness is a way of *being*. I made a commitment a long time ago that any time I passed a roadside stall run by a child,

I would stop and buy something. It didn't matter what they were selling. Because it's practising kindness. And that is something I want to emit from the inside, out.

To embody authenticity

How do you know you're authentic? Likely, you've been told. I've received the feedback myself countless times – when someone from my online community meets me for the first time in real life. 'You're exactly how you are online!' At first, it used to throw me – of course I was, isn't that the point? But as the years passed, I started to realise how rare this actually is – especially nowadays with the introduction of filters, algorithms, content strategies and online 'rules' of engagement (and growth). It can feel like such a hindrance to show up as the truth of who you are – the real, raw, vulnerable truth – when you also have a business to run or marketing strategies to execute. I get it. I guess for me – even as someone with a background in strategic marketing – nothing can ever override my truth. I post when I want to post. I share what I want to share. I don't use filters in my stories. I show up when I am unwell, I show up when I am sad, I show up when I am celebrating. I claim the full spectrum of my life online, and this has been one of my greatest successes. Because my community trusts me. They know that what they get from me is honesty. And for me you can't put a price on that.

An article in *Psychology Today* even references authenticity as pivotal when it comes to mental health – correlated with many aspects of psychological wellbeing, including vitality, self-esteem and coping skills.[46]

46 www.psychologytoday.com/au/basics/identity

I asked Britt to share how we can become more authentically ourselves, in the context of our relationship to our identity. She shared the teachings of Dr Brian Little (Professor of Personality Psychology at Berkeley), and summarised his four core elements of the self:

1. The biogenic self: The parts of us that come directly from our genetics, like hair colour, height, eye colour.
2. The sociogenic self: The parts of us that have been developed from the culture, environment and conditioning we grew up with. This might include the way we celebrate birthdays, our political beliefs, the kinds of foods we know how to cook, the way we learn to express our emotions.
3. The idiogenic self: The parts of us that come naturally to us. If no one was watching, and no one taught you how to do something, how would you *naturally* do it? How do you *naturally* prefer to decorate your home, dress, spend your time?
4. Your personal projects: The final piece to the identity pie is the most important and relieves us all of the belief that who we are is established or out of our hands. Your personal projects – that is, anything that you take on as a passion project (like my foray into local theatre, for example) – have the ability to shape you and your identity in a way that supersedes your biogenic, sociogenic and idiogenic selves. Your personal projects are the identity disruptor that we can all leverage to transform ourselves into whoever we wish to be.

ACTIVITY: **Be more you**

Here is an exercise from Britt, to really gauge an understanding of who you – authentically – are.

To understand who you really are, grab your journal and write each of the 'selves' at the top of a fresh page. Write down everything you can think of that would or could contribute to who you are at this moment. For example, write down every aspect of your genetics that contributes to your biogenic self. Write down every cultural, environmental and conditional experience you've lived through – good, bad or otherwise – that contributes to your biogenic self, and so on.

When you see all of the plentiful contributors to who you are, ideally you will develop compassion and deeper understanding for why you are so complex, multifaceted and, oftentimes, contradictory.

To embody authenticity, be more of you. All sides of you. The light and the shade. When someone asks you how you are, answer honestly. When people ask you to share parts of your life story, speak truthfully. When you're going through a hard time, let the people you love know. Notice the parts of you that cringe, or tell you you're attention-seeking. Maybe you are just desiring to be witnessed in a whole new deep and true way?

If you are genuinely yourself, people will feel it – just as much as you can tell when someone isn't being themselves. It doesn't pass the vibe check. It doesn't matter if you're claiming to be the most authentic person in the world. If you are mimicking, copying or simply embodying more of who you think you should be – it will be felt. Get to know YOU more. And then let that shine.

To cultivate confidence

This is a tough one. To a degree, I think you can be born with a healthy dose of confidence, especially if you have grown up in an environment that has encouraged safe and free expression of self. That said, like any trait we are wishing to embody more, confidence grows with practice. With stepping into the arena of our lives – centre stage – and turning the spotlight on, even among the fear and resistance. To grow in confidence, we have to practise being confident, to train ourselves to feel that it is safe to do so.

When I first went live on a social media platform, I was petrified. I knew this was a part of my confidence I wanted to grow – to be able to speak to large groups of people, on the spot – but my gosh was I still so afraid of what people thought of me. That said, I knew the only way out was through and so, one day, more than seven years ago now, I jumped onto my Facebook account, and hit the Live button. I still have access to that video today. My voice was shaky, my hands were trembling, and even my vocal tone was so different to how it is today. I was very obviously in fear. But I did it anyway. And once I moved through that hurdle, I kept doing it. I showed up week after week, eventually shifting from Facebook to Instagram and would go live every Monday morning (they were called my Monday Morning Musings for those who remember!). I went live once a week for years after that. And now, speaking in public, or live on my social media, doesn't make me nervous at all.

It lights me up. I find joy in the experience. Because I built my confidence.

It would be remiss of me to talk about confidence and not address body image here – given that I know this is a paramount subject matter that comes to mind, as women at least, when we consider where in our lives we would like to develop more confidence in ourselves. Unfortunately, it is a deep societal wounding that we hold around our worth being tied up in how we look. And as someone whose light both emits from embodying confidence in my body (as a model) and also someone who holds great fear around expressing her body (because of years of public trolling and abuse) I really understand how challenging this piece can be. And without writing a whole book on it (maybe that's for another day) – what I will say is this. The confidence I have recently developed in my body – especially in postpartum healing, alongside navigating the most unwell, and physically inflamed and swollen I have ever been – has been grounded in the notion of body neutrality. Not body love. Not body confidence. But coming to a place of feeling neutral about my body. Focusing on all the things my body CAN do, rather than what she can't (currently) do. Focusing on the features I do like about myself, rather than the things I am triggered by. And not forcing myself to get to an 'end goal' of: this is how I should feel always about my body. Just allowing myself to live alongside her, and experience the ebbs and flows of occupying her, without making it mean anything about me.

I dress beautifully because it makes me feel confident. And I equally dress like a slob because I'm needing a day where I don't leave the house. I do my hair and makeup because I love feeling put together. And I equally don't even brush my hair (I actually don't own a brush) or moisturise my face because I can't be fucked that day. I go through seasons where I'll get my nails done, and I'll go through seasons where the thought of sitting in a nail salon is literally anxiety-inducing. (I've even been trolled for my lack of pedicured toes on a red carpet once!)

This relaxed way of being in my body – letting myself do and have both, depending on how I am feeling in any given moment – is what has lent itself to my confidence. Because I feel neutral about her. It's changed the game for me.

To practise positivity

One of the biggest insights that came through when I asked the question *what makes someone shiny?* was in reference to positivity, and happiness. These people feel like sunshine to be around because their optimism radiates from the inside, out. And I really feel that this is the trait we lean on here: optimism. I know for me in the past, I have slapped on a happy face (I did this for many years) – because I knew being the 'happy one' was a mask I could wear when I was feeling anything but. It deterred people from having a peek at what was underneath. And the thing is, we are not supposed to feel happy all the time. If we are truly feeling our feelings – and moving them through – we will have moments of happiness met equally with moments of sadness, rage and grief. So no, the key here is not to be happy all the time.

But we CAN hold optimism, even among the challenges life sends our way. We can see life through the lens of glass half full. And to do this, we have to catch ourselves when we are playing in the opposite energy of this. We have to catch ourselves in victimhood.

When I was sitting in a therapy session recently, I was asked what my biggest challenges in other people were. I didn't realise this at the time, but what we were about to highlight were the mirrors other people reflected back to me, on my own shadowy traits. Without hesitation, I answered 'victimhood'. I feel uncomfortable when people play victim to the mishaps in their life, and don't do anything to change that. What actually ended up happening was my therapist and I unpacking all of the ways I was playing victim in my own life. And there were plenty. Where was I martyring myself in motherhood, because 'no one can look after my little girl like me'? Where was I not asking for help even though I really needed it, because I thought people should just show up and guess that I needed them? Where was I complaining about the same challenged relationship dynamic, but not actually doing anything to change it? Where was I bemoaning 'another health flare' but not actually resting as much as I needed to?

Victimhood dilutes our capacity to shine. Now this doesn't mean we can never 'play victim' again – far from it. I was super victim-y when we said goodbye to Archie and my health flared worse than it ever had before. It was an awful time, and I absolutely threw myself a pity party. But what matters here is that we recognise when we are doing it.

I will say to my friend, 'I just need to be a victim for a second, can I vent please?' and I get all of my victim vibes out. I whinge, I complain, I say, 'This isn't fair …' I might even shake it all out (somatic movement) and then … I'll choose what to do next. Victimhood lives in immobility, and we can challenge it with action. This is where optimism comes in.

A mantra that really got me through postpartum and those very dark days was this: *not forever, just for now*. Reminding myself that everything – literally every life experience – is a season. And when things are really, truly hard, can we remind ourselves that they aren't forever? Nothing ever is.

This isn't to bypass our pain – not at all – but it is to see life through the lens of lessons. Rather than asking *why is this happening to me?*, let's shift our lens to *what is this trying to teach me?* Can we remind ourselves of the impossibly challenging moments we've faced, and conquered, before – as a reference point of our strength and resilience? Rather than sitting in immovable hopelessness, can we invite in the help of a loved one we feel safe enough to lower our guard with, and ask them to hold us?

This is where our communities come right back around, because life will continue to throw us lessons, and spanners, and plot twists and, yep, our dreaded ego deaths. It's a rule of life. You cannot move through it without facing the seasonal highs and lows – and the sooner we can come to terms with this, the sooner we can realise life is not out to get us. But when we are surrounded by people who we feel safe with and can hold us through all of our seasons – the celebrations and the breakdowns in equal measure – then we are more likely to move through our hard seasons with a sense of liberation.

To embody your truth

It seems pretty obvious, but the first point here is to identify what your truth actually is. And for most of us – when asked this question – we can be absolutely thrown. What is your truth? What are the values you hold close to your heart? What is the legacy you wish to leave behind? How do you want your energy to leave people feeling?

These are all questions to ponder when deciphering how to show up more in your truth. And when your truth is embodied, vulnerability (another shiny trait) is a byproduct. Your truth is not slapping on an 'I'm okay' face because you don't want to burden anyone with your challenges. Your truth is not holding back your tears when they spring to your eyes because you're in a public place or, like me, being interviewed on a major podcast. Your truth is how genuinely you express all sides of you. To me, this is living in integrity.

You can make all of the claims you like in your Instagram bio, on your website, anywhere you describe yourself with words. But words are nothing if they are not embodied.

I have seen it time and time again. The born-again Christian who preaches love yet casts more judgement and self-righteousness than an atheist in the next room. The coach who teaches about the importance of showing up for your friendships yet chooses not to attend a friend's wedding, instead opting for a money-making opportunity that falls on the same day. The friendly, chirpy podcast host who speaks kindly over the airwaves, and awfully about people behind their backs.

Integrity is rooted in honesty and morality. It's walking your talk. In my experience, living with integrity at the forefront of my life has had me make some really challenging decisions.

For instance, as I shared in Chapter 6, earlier this year I decided that after seven years practicing as a psychic reader, it was time to close my books. Now, this decision made no sense – remember

I was making more money than ever, I was fully booked and had a waitlist out the door and I was really good at my job. But it felt out of alignment for me. Showing up for these sessions was no longer in integrity because my heart wasn't in it.

At the same time as writing this book, I had enlisted a designer to help me develop my first oracle card deck. I spent thousands of dollars on the designs and yet, somewhere along the way, I found that my heart wasn't in it anymore. So I stopped.

In both of these instances, I have said no to money – in fact, I've lost money – to say yes to my integrity. Because for me, living truthfully surpasses any level of income.

Integrity asks us to choose our hearts every single time. This can be a hard choice to make. But on the other side of living with integrity is a deeper embodiment of your truth – and this becomes a relatable, admirable and shiny aspect of who you are.

To dream big

My favourite ever aspect of shiny people: they are the dreamers. And because they dare to dream, they more often than not are living their dreams.

I have spent my whole life in the pursuit of a life beyond my wildest dreams. I think to a degree this level of optimism, expansion, 'anything is possible' energy is something we are born with. It's also something cultivated in childhood – for me, to dream was an escape from my painful upbringing. I would spend hours locked in my childhood bedroom writing about my greatest dreams and desires. In Year 10, a motivational speaker asked us to dream our biggest dream – and mine was to be Australia's answer to Oprah (still kind of is!).

Dreaming is my favourite thing. Casting a vision wide and trusting in what will land. This is where vision boarding has been an ultimate practice for me. I remember watching *The Secret* and having my mind blown at the manifestations of successful people. Today, so much of my life has been created from a baseline 'dreaming practice' with my vision boards. One example is back when I was in my corporate life, dreaming of a European holiday. I found a beautiful full-page image of a coastal town in Italy. I had no idea of the location, but I pasted it on my private vision board, which I didn't share with anyone else.

Two years passed by and I was on a European trip-of-a-lifetime with my then-boyfriend. It was on this trip – as we visited Vernazza, a coastal town in Italy – that Trent proposed. It wasn't until months after we returned from the trip, that I was sorting through my old journals and found that vision board. Pride of place was an image of Vernazza.

There is an element of magic to life that you simply cannot make up. And the shiniest people have learned how to work with, cultivate and amplify this magic. As I write this, I am facing my most recently curated vision board – words like 'shine on', 'beauty' and 'inspiration' stare back at me, as well as juxtaposed images of cut flower gardens, photo shoot sets, bookshelves, and yes – Oprah. I feel excited when I look at this board. Lit up. Inspired. And hold a deep knowing that what is meant for me – the biggest of my dreams – is all within reach. But we MUST let ourselves dream, first. That is the biggest starting point: to actually let ourselves go there. Desire the big, the bold, the audacious. To catch ourselves when we drop back into the limitations of 'what if I fail?'

And to remind ourselves that the only way to live a life beyond our wildest dreams is to dream it first, and then to go and DO IT.

We are the only person standing in our way. You are not only worthy and deserving of the brightest life of your dreams – but you owe it to yourself. To your loved ones. To your children. You owe it to them to live a life that is bright, and bold, and dream-like. To live this way is one of the most heart-centred and rebellious acts you can do. Because you are choosing to live a life of your own choosing. You are finally saying yes to you.

–

When I first started writing this book, I had no idea of the journey it would take me on. In the three months of writing, I have experienced some of the lowest health blows of my life. I have had to say goodbye to, and grieve, one of my beautiful dogs. I have spent weeks at a time in bed feeling immobilised by illness and fatigue. And yet, showing up to write this has kept me going. Because I know how important this work is.

This isn't just a book about being bright and shiny. This is a book about excavating all of the challenges you have been through – all of the life experiences you have let define you – and realising on the other side that you are SO MUCH MORE than the things that have happened, or are happening to you. You are the dreams you hold deep in your heart that you're too afraid to speak aloud, because that will make them real. You are the way your energy makes others feel when you are feeling at your best. You are the habits you practise daily, weekly, monthly to take extra care of yourself, because you know you are worthy of being cared for. You are all of the ripples of positive change you are cultivating in your life, that then ripple outward – to your children, your partner, your friends. You are so much more than where you have come from, and where you are headed. But sometimes – that little girl inside of us needs to be reminded. Of her worth. Of her beauty. Of her innate ability to shine. She needs to know that her dreams and her light have not been forgotten. We owe it to that little girl inside of us.

I found this entry in that very same journal I shared at the beginning of this book, written during one of the most difficult times of my life. I was only 13. I think there is something in these words for all of us:

> I keep thinking if when I'm older, I might look back in here to see what I was like as a kid. If so, hi future me! You better be doing something good with your life because you have the ability to do it. Go on – go out there and make your dreams come true! I believe in you! I don't want to end up unhappy in life. I want to be happy. To show the world who I am and what I can do. I want to help the world – make the sad, happy, the sick, better, the hungry, full. So future me, if you are reading this and you know you haven't done any of the above, go out and make it happen. Only you can control yourself, you are the only person with the ability to tell yourself what to do. Don't let anyone push you around. Don't let anyone tell you you can't make a difference. Go out there and prove them wrong! So that you can say to them – See? I'm Hollie Azzopardi and I said I could change the world. And look. I did.

Where to from Here?

I know that this is a lot to take in – I mean, I think we can all gather that a journey to healing will come with moments of intense highs and lows and everything in between. I've said it before and will say it repeatedly – this work is not a race. In fact, I ended my last book with the Doctor Phil (lol) quote: 'Life is a marathon, not a sprint'.

The same rule applies here. Your journey to saying yes to you is a lifelong one. This work is not a tick box to be applied once and forgotten forever. Below are some final points of reflection for you to visit time and time again. Not just when you come to the end of reading these pages, but also in any moment you feel disconnected from who you really are. Any moment of ego death, identity crumble or *why is this happening to me?* – I want you to remember these prompts. Because life will life. My hope is that, next time, you won't feel so alone in the process.

How can I go back to basics? What are three of the simplest, easiest practices I can pick up to tend to my nervous system right now?

- Ⓨ Ⓝ Am I drinking enough (good quality) water?
- Ⓨ Ⓝ Am I getting my morning sunlight?
- Ⓨ Ⓝ Am I getting adequate sleep?
- Ⓨ Ⓝ Am I following the simple nutritional guidelines for nervous system regulation?

If you answered no for any of the above, start here.
You can implement these to establish a baseline.

How can I slow down? Where does my body feel rushed, urgent or overwhelmed? How can I mitigate these feelings so I feel safe, grounded and slow?

Ⓨ Ⓝ Am I practising box breathing?

Ⓨ Ⓝ Am I journalling?

Ⓨ Ⓝ Am I listening to music?

Ⓨ Ⓝ Am I meditating?

Ⓨ Ⓝ Am I keeping my space/home clean?

Ⓨ Ⓝ Am I welcoming beauty into my home?

Ⓨ Ⓝ Have I practised EFT?

Ⓨ Ⓝ Have I considered booking time with a recommended chiropractor?

If you answered no for any of the above, start here. If there are multiple 'no's, pick one to start with and build from there. You can implement these as ongoing practices to slow down.

Where can I tune in? Where does my energetic body need tending to, as much as my mental and physical bodies?

- (Y) (N) Have I considered booking time with a somatic therapist, bodywork practitioner or TRE therapist?
- (Y) (N) Have I considered booking a reading with an astrologer or human design reader?
- (Y) (N) Have I been setting energetic boundaries?
- (Y) (N) Have I been communicating with my guides/spirit team?
- (Y) (N) Have I practised ecstatic movement/dance?
- (Y) (N) Have I practised vocal toning?
- (Y) (N) Have I used scent as an anchor?
- (Y) (N) Have I set up a ritual space/altar for myself?
- (Y) (N) Have I sat with cacao/set intention/prayed?

If you answered no for any of the above, start here. If there are multiple 'no's, pick one to start with that feels truest to you and focus on that. Anything that feels too stretchy or uncomfortable does not need your time or attention; just focus on what feels appealing to you.

Where can I shine? What do I need to process or unravel, to step more into who I came here to be?

- (Y) (N) Do I feel celebrated by the people in my life?
- (Y) (N) Have I celebrated someone in my life recently?
- (Y) (N) Do I feel safe to be the full version of me with the company I keep?
- (Y) (N) Do I have a creative and/or community outlet that allows me to fully show up as exactly who I am?
- (Y) (N) Have I created something for the joy of it, and shared it with others even if it made me cringe?
- (Y) (N) Do I have identity diversity currently? (See page 174)
- (Y) (N) Am I taking regular action steps in pursuing my dream life, even when the fear of failure arises?
- (Y) (N) Am I practising kindness, fully, with myself and others?
- (Y) (N) Am I showing up authentically, with every connection and on every online platform?
- (Y) (N) Am I practising optimism?
- (Y) (N) Am I embodying my truth?
- (Y) (N) Am I letting myself dream?
- (Y) (N) Have I created a vision board?

If you answered no for any of the above, start here. If there are multiple 'no's, pick one to start with that feels like the 'stickiest', or the most charged, and seek support in the form of a therapist, coach, kinesiologist or similar to help work on this piece for you. These are the big, deeply rooted beliefs that often take the most work. Be gentle with yourself as you navigate these unravellings with someone you trust.

Acknowledgements

'Be careful what you wish for', or so the saying goes. I can confidently say that this applies to writing. 'Be careful what you write for' has been my reality twice over now, with both of my books taking me to places I never anticipated, all in the name of practising what I preach. This book, especially, took me to some of the most difficult, dark and challenging moments of my life so far – not just in revisiting moments, but in living new ones as I wrote.

I wrote this book between spells of intense physical illness that left me bedridden for weeks at a time; I did a large chunk of writing while also grieving our dog Archie Rose; and much of the editing took place while living in our friend's garage and then in a caravan on our land, as I had nowhere else to go. (A story for another time, I'm sure.) There were countless people who stepped in and stepped up for me and my family during this time, and I want to be sure some key people are recognised for just how important their support was – not just as I wrote this book, but also as I re-established what it meant to be loved in a way that was unconditional and safe.

Cass – I don't know what I would have done without your unwavering support, both throughout this writing process and also during our intense initiations into motherhood. Spending six weeks living in your home was one of the greatest gifts you could have given me in every way. Jordan and Asher, thank you both too – you are our family and I am forever grateful.

Liv and Benny, thank you for offering Clarry the Caravan as a last-resort home option, and for showing my family what is possible when it comes to cultivating a home that is both beautiful and healing.

To the many, many healers, energy workers and women who would have likely been burned in former lives for their gifts and wisdom, but without whom I wouldn't have been able to navigate this season of healing: Britt, Zoe, Asha, Simone, Karen, Jules, Sandy, Megan, Emily, Chantel, Erin. Thank you for shining in the powerful ways you do. The world needs your gifts and your work. Never stop.

To my beautiful friends and family, of which I am lucky to have too many to name – you know who you are. A special acknowledgement to Carmen, Leah, Jess (Jric), Em and Jess (Mutti) for being my support system from well before life took me on the wild journey I'm now living. Thank you for being there from the very start. To Britt, for holding me through countless voice notes as I wrote and as we navigated our signature mirroring lives. Grateful doesn't even begin to cover it.

To my theatre family, for showing me light and healing in a way I never anticipated. Bobbie – co-producing alongside you was a dream come true because of the friendship it gave me in you.

To the beautiful Affirm Press team. Kelly – thank you for seeing the potential of this book in me. It is such a gift to work with you, and the entire team. To Zoe and Laura – editing alongside you both was a joy. A huge thank you to the wonderful contributors to this book – people I admire for their wisdom and insights. It's an honour to share these pages with you.

To those of you who are part of my extended community: my clients, online community, Heart Space members, *Soul Talk* listeners and readers of my first book. Words will never express what it means to have your love and support. Simply put: you help make my dreams come true. Thank you.

To the women I have come from: my mum, my grandma, my nanna, and their mothers, and theirs. I will forever walk in a way that is honouring the legacy and path you have paved for me and my little girl.

To my little brother and little sister, Ty and Carmz. Ma bro and ma sis. No one will ever really comprehend what we navigated together growing up, but it brings my heart such gratitude to have had you both through it all. I'm so proud of you both and the people you have become. I love you with all of my heart.

To our nanny, Sharni, for caring for my little queen while I wrote. I genuinely wouldn't have been able to write this book without you. Thank you for caring for her the way you do.

To my beautiful little family: Trenny, Little Girl and Lola. This year has been one of the hardest. Grieving our little man was never something we wanted, especially at the same time as navigating my health and our home challenges. Trenny, I couldn't do most of what I do in my life without your stoic, unwavering support right by my side. Words will never be enough to thank you. I love you.

Little Girl – everything I do, every word I write, every wound I heal is for you. You are a gift to the world, my girl. My wish is that you forever take up space in the big, bold and shiny ways you do. You are loved. You are safe. Mummy's got you x